The
Least
You Should Know about
English

TEST
BOOKLET

NINTH EDITION

Paige Wilson

Pasadena City College

THOMSON

✦

™

WADSWORTH

Australia · Canada · Mexico · Singapore · Spain · United Kingdom · United States

THOMSON

WADSWORTH

The Least You Should Know about English, Test Booklet, Ninth Edition
Paige Wilson

Publisher: *Michael Rosenberg*
Acquisitions Editor: *Stephen Dalphin*
Editorial Assistant: *Cheryl Forman*
Marketing Manager: *Mary Jo Southern*
Marketing Assistant: *Dawn Giovanniello*
Advertising Project Manager: *Shemika Britt*
Editorial Production Manager: *Michael Burggren*

Manufacturing Manager: *Marcia Locke*
Permissions Editor: *Sarah Harkrader*
Technology Project Manager: *Joe Gallagher*
Production Service/Compositor: *Rozi Harris, Interactive Composition Corporation*
Cover Designer: *Gina Petti*
Printer: *Globus Printing*

Printed in the United States of America
1 2 3 4 5 6 7 09 08 07 06 05

For more information about our products, contact us at:
Thomson Learning Academic Resource Center
1-800-423-0563
For permission to use material from this text or product, submit a request online at
http://www.thomsonrights.com
Any additional questions about permissions can be submitted by email to
thomsonrights@thomson.com

Thomson Higher Education
25 Thomson Place
Boston, MA 02210-1202
USA

Asia (including India)
Thomson Learning
5 Shenton Way
#01-01 UIC Building
Singapore 068808

Australia/New Zealand
Thomson Learning Australia
102 Dodds Street
Southbank, Victoria 3006
Australia

Canada
Thomson Nelson
1120 Birchmount Road
Toronto, Ontario M1K 5G4
Canada

UK/Europe/Middle East/Africa
Thomson Learning
High Holborn House
50–51 Bedford Road
London WC1R 4LR
United Kingdom

ISBN 1-4130-0895-X

List of Tests

To the Instructor

This packet contains tests to accompany all three forms of *The Least You Should Know about English*.

The Pretest and Posttest will help determine students' progress. The rest of the tests may be used either as additional exercises to supplement those in the book or as competency tests. Answers to these tests are provided in the back of this packet only, not in the book itself.

1. Pretest   Part A

_____

Circle the correct word in each set of parentheses.

1. I'll make an outline first; (than, then) I'll fill in the details later.

2. (They're, Their, There) going to the parade early to get their favorite seats.

3. The amount of light affects indoor plants more (than, then) outdoor plants.

4. My health book has a picture of a marathon runner on (it's, its) cover.

5. The teacher's keys were (lying, laying) on the front desk, but he didn't see them.

6. My friends and I feel (good, well) about our projects.

7. Her new apartment is even smaller than both of her (brother's, brothers') apartments.

8. My counselor (could'nt, couldn't) see me today; he was too busy.

9. She has helped me many times before; I hope she can (help, helps) me again.

10. I (use, used) to know that poem by heart, but now I have forgotten most of it.

11. We have (gone, went) on the same vacation every summer since I was ten.

12. The windows in that room (is, are) too small, so the light at our desks is very dim.

13. Scholarships (offer, offers) help for all kinds of students.

14. Two members of the committee (has, have) already agreed to sign the petition.

15. A strong thesis and clear topic sentences (is, are) necessary for a strong essay.

16. The new math tutor helped Mark and (I, me) prepare for the upcoming test.

17. The only student who hadn't finished the project was (he, him).

18. Her classmates may be older, but they aren't as mature as (she, her).

19. Most of (we, us) students are still trying to complete our core classes.

20. My sister and (I, me) both received the same chain letter.

1.   Pretest   Part B   _____

Each of the following sentences demonstrates an error listed below. Identify the error by placing the appropriate letter in the blank. Then revise the sentence to correct the error.

    a. misused adjective or adverb

    b. fragment

    c. run-on sentence

    d. subject-verb agreement error

    e. shift in time or person

    f. misplaced or dangling modifier

    g. faulty parallel structure

21. ____ As I was driving home from work, my sister calls me on my cell phone.

22. ____ Students who participate in class and do their homework on time.

23. ____ The deadline was approaching but we shortened our outlines and finished on time.

24. ____ Our room at the ski lodge was the larger of the three.

25. ____ My counselor understand some of the problems I have.

26. ____ I don't understand some of my friends; you never know what they're thinking.

27. ____ This room needs better windows, more desks, and to be cleaned thoroughly.

28. ____ Taking as much time as necessary on each of the test questions.

29. ____ They felt badly about forgetting my birthday.

30. ____ Without a jacket, the wind was freezing.

1.   Pretest   Part C   _____

Rewrite the following sentences to include the necessary punctuation
(, ; : . ! ? ' " " ___) and capital letters.

31.   i dont know whether i should apply for a loan or not

32.   mr branford always writes positive comments on my homework

33.   she has read the book the house on mango street four times

34.   a person who was born before 1990 can still qualify for that license

35.   janet who was born on february 10 1989 can still qualify for that license

36.   will you figure out the taxes this year or do you want me to do it

37.   katharine lee bates wrote the words to america the beautiful

38.   whenever my mom gets home from work she smiles in a special way

39.   a basic first-aid kit has the following items bandages medicines and instructions

40.   the childrens center is next to the womens gym

2. Words Often Confused   Test A   _____

Circle the correct word in each set of parentheses.

1. I waited in line for (a, an) hour to buy (a, an) history textbook and a new pen.

2. A good friend will offer (advise, advice) and (accept, except) criticism.

3. Scary movies only (affect, effect) me when the special (affects, effects) are unexpected.

4. We were (all ready, already) to take the test when (are, our) teacher arrived.

5. During the summer (brake, break), I will fix the (brakes, breaks) on my car.

6. Yesterday, I (choose, chose) special (clothes, cloths) for my interview.

7. That miniature golf (coarse, course) uses (coarse, course) sand for the walkways.

8. I always (chose, choose) colors that (complement, compliment) my mood.

9. He blushes when he receives (a, an) heartfelt (complement, compliment).

10. A person's (conscious, conscience) develops (it's, its) quality over time.

11. We went camping in the (dessert, desert) with little food and no (dessert, desert).

12. I (feel, fill) good about the paper that is (do, due) tomorrow.

13. You should (have, of) seen my dog walking back and (fourth, forth) for hours.

14. I drove my new car to school today; (it's, its) (hear, here) in the parking lot.

15. With so much (knew, new) technology, we all must (know, no) several passwords.

2. Words Often Confused   Test B   _____

Circle the correct word in each set of parentheses.

1.   The (lead, led) in this pencil always comes (loose, lose).

2.   The firefighters (lead, led) everyone in the building (passed, past) the smoke.

3.   The (personal, personnel) office has all of my (personal, personnel) information.

4.   A dove is just one symbol for (piece, peace); (they're, their, there) are many others.

5.   The (principal, principle) of my high school was (quiet, quite) tall.

6.   I (right, write) with my (right, write) hand, but I paint with my left hand.

7.   (They're, Their, There) garage is much roomier (than, then) ours.

8.   At first, (they're, their, there) were three birds; (than, then) two of them flew away.

9.   The children (threw, through) several balls (threw, through) the holes in the net.

10. He's (two, too, to) busy (two, too, to) relax because he's taking (two, too, to) math classes.

11. I don't know (weather, whether) it will be sunny (were, wear, where) you live or not.

12. (Who's, Whose) costume will she (were, wear, where) in that play?

13. The (woman, women) on the left is the one (who's, whose) teaching the yoga class.

14. Have you (passed, past) all of (you're, your) science tests?

15. (You're, Your) making plans to transfer, aren't you?

2. Words Often Confused   Test C   _____

Circle the correct word in each set of parentheses.

1. (Do, Due) to bad (weather, whether), our trip to the mountains has been postponed.

2. Peanuts (are, our) snacks that can cause serious side (affects, effects) due to allergies.

3. (They're, Their, There) hoping that they don't finish in (fourth, forth) place.

4. The (dessert, desert) looks beautiful with (it's, its) cactus flowers all in bloom.

5. Yesterday, they (choose, chose) the colors for (they're, their, there) wedding.

6. The (woman, women) at the center of the controversy might (loose, lose) her job.

7. You should (have, of) heard about (you're, your) application by now.

8. Counselors often (advise, advice) students (two, too, to) wait before choosing a major.

9. (It's, Its) supposed to be (quiet, quite) in the library.

10. Everyone has a new book (accept, except) the teacher, (who's, whose) copy is old and worn.

11. In (a, an) underground parking lot, (it's, its) easy to feel lost.

12. The (brakes, breaks) on the bus (were, wear, where) starting to squeak.

13. If (two, too, to) clubs have meetings on the same day, (than, then) one should reschedule.

14. Ms. Jones (complemented, complimented) me; she said, "You (right, write) with a clear voice."

15. I (passed, past) my driving test and drove (passed, past) my friend's house to show off.

3. Parts of Speech   Test A   _____

Use the abbreviations **n**, **pro**, **v**, **adj**, **adv**, **prep**, **conj**, and **interj** to label the parts of speech above the words in the following sentences. You may ignore the words *a*, *an*, and *the*, which are special adjectives called *articles*.

1. I researched my topic on the Internet.

2. Everyone on the team has the same goal.

3. The post office is very busy during the holidays.

4. I met someone from my hometown.

5. Coffee and tea taste completely different.

6. You always tell such interesting stories.

7. I laugh whenever I remember that scene.

8. The people at the back of the line shared a pepperoni pizza.

9. The library steps need a better railing.

10. I hope that the weather improves soon.

11. Walking to school is good exercise.

12. Frank sleeps better during the day, so he works at night.

13. No, my car does not need new tires.

14. Happiness usually arrives unexpectedly.

15. We found two baby squirrels in a hollow log.

n   = noun
pro   = pronoun
v   = verb
adj   = adjective
adv   = adverb
prep   = preposition
conj   = conjunction
interj = interjection

3. Parts of Speech   Test B   _____

Use the abbreviations **n**, **pro**, **v**, **adj**, **adv**, **prep**, **conj**, and **interj** to label the parts of speech above the words in the following sentences. You may ignore the words *a*, *an*, and *the*, which are special adjectives called *articles*.

1.   Tennis is a popular outdoor sport.

2.   His English teacher assigned a research paper.

3.   Movies and television are only two forms of entertainment.

4.   One pickle tastes like every other pickle to him.

5.   The highly polished silverware sparkled on the table.

6.   While the children played, the adults talked about politics.

7.   They will accept a letter of recommendation or a personal essay.

8.   Five people were sitting in the waiting room.

9.   Scientists have discovered new information about dinosaurs.

10.   Did you send him a real letter or an email?

11.   Paper money has become more colorful recently.

12.   Ouch! That application gave me a paper cut.

13.   Hal and Trudy sang as they drove up the coast.

14.   We should go on picnics more often.

15.   That restaurant's food is much too spicy for most people.

n	= noun
pro	= pronoun
v	= verb
adj	= adjective
adv	= adverb
prep	= preposition
conj	= conjunction
interj	= interjection

3. Parts of Speech   Test C   _____

Use the abbreviations **n**, **pro**, **v**, **adj**, **adv**, **prep**, **conj**, and **interj** to label the parts of speech above the words in the following sentences. You may ignore the words *a*, *an*, and *the*, which are special adjectives called *articles*.

1. Heavy rains caused flooding in the valleys and in the mountains.
2. Our uniforms included light gray pants and simple white shirts.
3. Everyone knows that blue and yellow make green.
4. Lisa has become a well-known pastry chef.
5. A smile is a very revealing facial expression.
6. Vegans are vegetarians who do not eat or use any animal products.
7. The students in the singing class sang a new song.
8. Then they sang it again.
9. Everyone on our block has a party in the summer.
10. You can travel with us if you get your passport.
11. European vacations can be very expensive.
12. Jonathan quietly answered the doctor's questions.
13. Candice received a basket of gourmet foods for her birthday.
14. The football players ran onto the field as the music played.
15. Ten people were standing in line at the Indian restaurant.

n	= noun
pro	= pronoun
v	= verb
adj	= adjective
adv	= adverb
prep	= preposition
conj	= conjunction
interj	= interjection

4.   Adjectives and Adverbs   Test A   _____

Identify whether the word *early* or *late* is used as an adjective or an adverb in each sentence.

1.   I have an *early* class in the morning. (adjective, adverb)

2.   Whenever I wake up *late*, I have a bad day. (adjective, adverb)

3.   *Early* students usually get the best seats. (adjective, adverb)

4.   Heavy packages are usually delivered *late* in the day. (adjective, adverb)

5.   Some teachers don't accept *late* papers. (adjective, adverb)

6.   The teacher's assistant always arrives *early*. (adjective, adverb)

7.   Pain in the joints can be an *early* symptom of the flu. (adjective, adverb)

8.   *Late* proposals will not be accepted. (adjective, adverb)

9.   Most of the *early* applicants received scholarships. (adjective, adverb)

10.   My daughter fell asleep *early* last night. (adjective, adverb)

11.   An *early* warning system can help in an emergency. (adjective, adverb)

12.   I watched an *early* broadcast of the local news. (adjective, adverb)

13.   Our train was *late*, so we waited for an hour in the lobby. (adjective, adverb)

14.   We both submitted our essays *early* and received extra credit. (adjective, adverb)

15.   My neighbor planted his flowers too *late* in the season. (adjective, adverb)

4.   Adjectives and Adverbs   Test B   _____

Identify whether the *italicized* word is used as an adjective or an adverb in each sentence.

1.   A *good* swimmer can tread water for a long time. (adjective, adverb)

2.   In the afternoon, my older brother *often* takes a nap. (adjective, adverb)

3.   The *parking* situation has improved lately. (adjective, adverb)

4.   I found a parking space easily *yesterday*. (adjective, adverb)

5.   Your advice is very *valuable* to me. (adjective, adverb)

6.   The red sauce was *spicier* than the green sauce. (adjective, adverb)

7.   My friend delivered his speech *quite* loudly. (adjective, adverb)

8.   I feel *happy* about my decision. (adjective, adverb)

9.   Songs can trigger *many* memories. (adjective, adverb)

10.   They need to buy a more *powerful* computer. (adjective, adverb)

11.   My cousin has knit several scarves *recently*. (adjective, adverb)

12.   *Tuesday's* homework included forty pages of reading. (adjective, adverb)

13.   Six *talented* people performed all of the parts in that play. (adjective, adverb)

14.   We cut the potatoes into chunks and *then* soaked them in water. (adjective, adverb)

15.   The ladder was *too* short to reach the ceiling. (adjective, adverb)

4. Adjectives and Adverbs   Test C   _____

Label the adjectives (**adj**) and adverbs (**adv**) in the following sentences. You may ignore the words *a*, *an*, and *the*, which are special adjectives called *articles*.

1. My counselor is a very nice person.

2. Our teacher usually begins the class with a short lecture.

3. Fancy mice can be good pets for some people.

4. The next train leaves in exactly ten minutes.

5. The peach pie was too sweet for me.

6. One ticket to that amusement park costs fifty dollars.

7. I became extremely sleepy during the piano recital.

8. He does not have any clear transfer plans yet.

9. The room's furniture included one couch, two chairs, and a coffee table.

10. The lime green curtains gave the room an eerie glow.

11. I always reply to your emails very quickly.

12. Do you want our old air conditioner?

13. The morning air felt so crisp in the mountains.

14. My cell phone is smaller than your cell phone.

15. Jake has the tiniest cell phone of all.

5. Contractions and Possessives   Test A   _____

Circle the correct form of contraction or possessive in each sentence.

1.   (Who's, Whose) driving with us to Las Vegas?

2.   My car has a slow leak in one of (it's, its) tires.

3.   Potatoes should be thrown away if (they're, their) green inside.

4.   I am glad that (it's, its) almost summer.

5.   A (puppy's, puppies') attention span can be very short.

6.   (You're, Your) taking too many classes this semester.

7.   When (it's, its) raining, people should drive more carefully.

8.   Shoppers who check (they're, their) receipts often find errors.

9.   Airports are good places to study (people's, peoples') behavior.

10.   (Children's, Childrens') toys have to pass many safety tests.

11.   The (girl's, girls') backpacks were lined up behind their desks.

12.   Our (mail carrier's, mail carriers') bag fell out of the truck yesterday.

13.   Have you received (you're, your) grades for last semester yet?

14.   Those (are'nt, aren't) the right ingredients for stew.

15.   Some of those classes meet in the (men's, mens') gym.

5. Contractions and Possessives   Test B   _____

Circle the correct form of contraction or possessive in each set of parentheses.

1. A (book's, books') title can have an impact on (it's, its) sales.

2. (They're, Their) happy because (they're, their) daughter just graduated from law school.

3. That (house's, houses') porch is large and beautiful, but (it's, its) living room is too small.

4. My (cousin's, cousins') car is a convertible, and (it's, its) bright red.

5. (Who's, Whose) planning our (company's, companies') summer picnic this year?

6. I took my best (friend's, friends') advice and (did'nt, didn't) buy a used computer.

7. (It's, Its) fascinating to learn about different (country's, countries') flags.

8. Little (boy's, boys') shoes and little (girl's, girls') shoes are usually very different.

9. (Men's, Mens') athletic shoes and (women's, womens') athletic shoes are more similar.

10. My math (teacher's, teachers') office has a funny cartoon on (it's, its) door.

11. All of the (student's, students') books and papers were on (they're, their) desks.

12. This (semester's, semesters') holidays all fall on Mondays; (is'nt, isn't) that odd?

13. (You're, Your) the one (who's, whose) interested in new scientific discoveries.

14. Students often (do'nt, don't) know (who's, whose) advice to take.

15. Last (week's, weeks') homework was collected by the (teacher's, teachers') aide.

5. Contractions and Possessives Test C _____

Circle the correct word in parentheses, and combine *italicized* words to form contractions.

1. Each herb has (it's, its) own smell; *it is* not hard to tell the difference.

2. *They are* planning to go to Europe for (their, there) honeymoon.

3. The mechanic looked at my (dad's, dads') car; *it has* been giving him trouble lately.

4. (Cat's, Cats') personalities *are not* all the same.

5. The (judge's, judges') decision was final, and the loser *was not* allowed to ask questions.

6. *I am* working with a microscope now, but I can't see through (it's, its) eye piece.

7. *They have* tried to anticipate all of the (student's, students') needs.

8. She *could not* see her (brother's, brothers') car anywhere in the parking lot.

9. *There is* a balloon on the roof of the (Smith's, Smiths') house.

10. He *was not* prepared for the substitute (teacher's, teachers') quiz.

11. Many of that (athlete's, athletes') scores *should have* been higher.

12. *You are* not the only one (who's, whose) feet hurt.

13. *What is* the zip code for the (Tomlin's, Tomlins') new address?

14. I *could have* printed my essay in the (school's, schools') computer lab.

15. The (city's, citys') smog problem *is not* as bad as it used to be.

6. Subjects and Verbs   Test A   _____

Underline the subjects and <u>double underline</u> the verbs in the following sentences.
Remember that a sentence may have more than one subject and more than one verb.

1. I wrote several new entries in my journal.

2. She takes two classes and works part-time.

3. A box of paper sat in the hallway for three days.

4. At the beginning of the semester, students wait in long lines at the bookstore.

5. Our remote control fell under the couch and disappeared.

6. Bowling is very good exercise.

7. The library contains books, magazines, newspapers, and other formats of information.

8. Canned pineapple, pears, and peaches taste delicious at any time of year.

9. Many of my friends call me on the weekends.

10. Without instructions, they assembled the cabinet and placed their television on top of it.

11. We studied together and talked about life.

12. All of the tables have six chairs.

13. The school's new schedule is an improvement.

14. We listened to the speaker and took notes in the dark.

15. The desks and the chalkboard are clean but need repair.

6.   Subjects and Verbs   Test B   _____

Underline the subjects and double underline the verbs in the following sentences. Remember that subjects sometimes come *after* verbs. If the subject *you* is *understood*, write it in the margin and underline it.

1.   Under the porch sat a little lost dog.

2.   There are two methods for payment.

3.   Cheese is a popular snack at parties.

4.   Mail me one copy of the receipt.

5.   Here are several photos from the reunion.

6.   There is a good reason for his behavior.

7.   Inside the shop was a beautiful assortment of pastries.

8.   Gather your notes for our meeting.

9.   There were two boats on the lake today.

10.   Towels in hotels are always too small.

11.   Be careful with your passwords.

12.   That is a classic yoga exercise.

13.   Near the window stood two artificial potted plants.

14.   Knead the bread dough for eight minutes.

15.   Sort all of the files alphabetically.

6. Subjects and Verbs   Test C   _____

Underline the subjects and double underline the verbs in the following sentences. Watch for more than one subject or more than one verb. Remember that subjects sometimes come *after* verbs. If the subject *you* is *understood*, write it in the margin and underline it.

1. His high school math teacher lives next door to him.
2. There are several buildings with balconies on our block.
3. People abandoned their cars in the traffic jam.
4. Look under the welcome mat for the key to my house.
5. Adults and children require different doses of medicine.
6. Take the freeway to its end and turn left.
7. Someone's alarm rang all night and bothered everyone in the neighborhood.
8. Inside the plastic bags were several kinds of snacks.
9. There is a full moon in the sky tonight.
10. Sugar, butter, and flour are the only ingredients in the dough.
11. Send me an email tomorrow.
12. A lizard jumped off a rock and scared the hikers.
13. Six of the twelve eggs broke in the pan.
14. Drawing and singing are two very admirable talents.
15. Toast the marshmallows slowly for the fullest flavor.

7. Phrases   Test A

_____

Put parentheses ( ) around any prepositional phrases in the following sentences. Remember that a prepositional phrase always begins with a preposition (such as *of, in, to, with, at, after, under, against, for,* or *during*) and ends with a noun or pronoun. A sentence may have one or more prepositional phrases or none at all.

1.   Examples and charts in textbooks can be very helpful.

2.   We met at a conference about safety.

3.   The last part of his address causes confusion for everyone.

4.   For dinner on Sunday, they ate hamburgers with fries.

5.   Yesterday, she and I took the placement test together.

6.   Thanksgiving is the last Thursday in November.

7.   He spoke to me quietly during the film.

8.   After the fire drill, everyone met in the cafeteria for coffee.

9.   I feel too vulnerable without a service contract for my computer.

10.   I acted as the judge in a mock trial at my school.

11.   Customers sit on benches at that restaurant.

12.   A blimp hovered in the sky above the football stadium.

13.   I found the expiration date on the bottom of the can.

14.   Words in one language often sound like words in other languages.

15.   The front of that phone opens with a little click.

7. Phrases Test B _____

First, <u>double underline</u> the real verbs in the following sentences. Then put brackets [ ] around the verbal phrases. Remember that verbals have three forms: 1) the "ing" form, 2) the "to ___" form, and 3) the "ed," "en," or "t" form and that they are never the real verbs in sentences. Each sentence in this test includes one verbal phrase.

1.   He enjoys playing the guitar.

2.   They need to complete their applications.

3.   Taken by a professional photographer, the graduation pictures pleased everyone.

4.   I saw my friend waiting in line at the gas station.

5.   Most people like to receive compliments.

6.   However, receiving gifts makes some people uncomfortable.

7.   She really wants to support the team.

8.   Choosing the right major takes time.

9.   They tried to improve their credit score.

10.   I sometimes visualize us traveling across Europe.

11.   The students chosen for that project were the best.

12.   Built in 1951, our house is in vogue right now.

13.   I want to walk a lot before my trip.

14.   We ate our individual pizzas slowly, enjoying every bite.

15.   Olympic athletes love to get gold medals.

7.   Phrases   Test C   _____

First, <u>double underline</u> the real verbs in the following sentences. Then put parentheses ( ) around prepositional phrases and brackets [ ] around verbal phrases. The two types of phrases may overlap, but remember to place the opening mark before the preposition or verbal that starts each phrase, and then include all the words that go with it. This test will be a challenge.

1. I like to have a break between classes.
2. Helped by the teacher's assistant, the students did well on that essay.
3. We went home without taking any pictures of the volcano.
4. My family needs to watch less television during the week.
5. Eaten in large quantities, black licorice can be dangerous.
6. Seen from a distance, the clouds seemed small and harmless.
7. In the first paragraph, try to state your main idea.
8. I like going to the movies with my friends.
9. You deserve an award for following the directions so closely.
10. The object of the game is to score the highest number of points.
11. He enjoys making his own bread and sharing it with others.
12. The pictures taken by that photographer were the best in the gallery.
13. Written in pencil, the letter was difficult to read without a strong light.
14. Loaded with vitamin C, tomatoes are good for most people.
15. Given a real bath by the kennel staff, my dog looked clean and smelled fresh.

8. Clauses   Test A   _____

Each of these sentences contains two clauses—one independent and one dependent. Place a dotted underline beneath the dependent clause in each sentence. Remember that dependent clauses begin with words such as *when, since, because, although, who, which,* or *that* and that they may be at the beginning, in the middle, or at the end of the sentence.

1. Whenever Ms. Stark asks a question, she looks at the ceiling.
2. He dropped his biology class because it conflicted with his work schedule.
3. I know what you mean.
4. We liked the movie until we read the review.
5. When she eats shrimp, she sometimes has an allergic reaction.
6. The athlete who wins the most medals gets the most television coverage.
7. As the actor turned toward the audience, he sneezed.
8. Someone who knows your password accessed your email yesterday.
9. Professor Talbot, whom we all know, received an award.
10. Before the curtain opens, someone checks all of the scenery.
11. She noticed that the corner of the couch had a rip at the bottom.
12. The party was a success because the guests knew each other well.
13. After the rainy season ends, the weather here is perfect.
14. I know many people who exercise regularly.
15. Do you know where their house is?

8. Clauses   Test B

Each of these sentences contains two or more clauses—one independent and at least one dependent. Place a <u>dotted underline</u> beneath all of the dependent clauses. Remember that dependent clauses begin with words like *when, since, because, although, who, which,* or *that* and that they may be at the beginning, in the middle, or at the end of the sentence.

1. As I ate my lunch at the park, a bird that lived in a tree flew down onto my bench.

2. Do you know anyone who builds kitchen cabinets?

3. Because he needed the key to the classroom, the substitute called the security office.

4. Wherever we went in Paris, we saw dogs who reminded us of our puppy back at home.

5. Nobody knows who took the basket.

6. Many people wish that they lived at a different time in history.

7. I saw that movie when I was in elementary school.

8. The homework that we had last week was actually fun.

9. Unless it rains on Sunday, the field trip will proceed as we planned.

10. One helicopter landed on top of the mountain just as another one took off.

11. The bells ring only while classes are in session.

12. After I took a nap, I felt so much better that I finished all of my homework.

13. You are taller than I am, and she is taller than you are.

14. Although I know that I can't afford it, I want to take a trip around the world.

15. Professional actors and musicians never give up once they have begun a performance.

8. Clauses   Test C   _____

Each of these sentences contains two or more clauses—one independent and at least one dependent. Place a dotted underline beneath all of the dependent clauses. Remember that dependent clauses begin with words like *when, since, because, although, who, which,* or *that* and that they may be at the beginning, in the middle, or at the end of the sentence.

1. In high school, I wrote an essay that won an award.
2. Once he received his tickets, he exchanged them for seats that were closer to the stage.
3. During the debate, I supported whatever my team proposed.
4. The novel that we read includes several characters who change for the better.
5. People who read newspapers know more about the candidates who are on the ballot.
6. No one shares his time more freely than he does.
7. Everyone noticed that the scenery was stuck and that the actors were nervous.
8. Until the rain arrives, we should use sprinklers that are controlled by a timer.
9. Whenever I need extra money, I work more hours.
10. The tuxedos that we rented required a large deposit because they were fancy.
11. Ice dancing is a sport that demands both physical ability and courage.
12. Since you missed class last week, you are a little behind in the project that we started.
13. We will be satisfied with whatever happens because we know that we studied.
14. Many believe that horses know when a person is afraid.
15. Since I love to drive, I am glad that long road trips are popular again.

9. Fragments   Test A   _____

Some of the word groups below are sentences, and some are phrase fragments. Write "correct" next to the sentences. Then revise the phrase fragments to form complete sentences. Remember that phrase fragments are incomplete sentences because they are missing a subject or a real verb—or both.

1. Eating too many sweets during the holidays.

2. I found the pliers at the bottom of the drawer.

3. That famous writer with the unusual name.

4. Because of the cold weather and the harsh winds.

5. Due to the power outage, my boss closed the store early.

6. The most comfortable chairs in their whole house.

7. The newest pens with erasable ink.

8. Talk with a counselor before choosing your major.

9. Causing a lot of problems for people at the concert.

10. I enjoy traveling in the summer with my family.

11. Creating stencil designs on my computer.

12. The stairs in the library and the ramps in the parking structure.

13. The fabric for the auditorium curtains arrived today.

14. Taking aspirin can help some people with heart problems.

15. Peaches and pears being summer fruits.

9. Fragments   Test B   _____

Some of the word groups below are sentences, and some are dependent clause fragments. Write "correct" next to the sentences. Then revise the dependent clause fragments to form complete sentences. Remember that dependent clause fragments are incomplete sentences because, even though they do have a subject and verb, they do not state a complete thought.

1.   Because organic eggs are now available in most stores.

2.   Because we hurried, we arrived just in time for the matinee.

3.   The test that the substitute teacher gave.

4.   In the morning when the sun shines and I listen to my favorite radio shows.

5.   On weekends, he practices whenever he can.

6.   When I was a volunteer and helped with the relief efforts.

7.   When you write an essay based on sources from the library or the Internet.

8.   Birds fly so gracefully that it looks easy.

9.   The parakeet that we had when I was growing up.

10.   Until the semester is over and I get my final grades.

11.   Write a paragraph about your favorite song.

12.   Why mosquitoes are attracted to some people more than others.

13.   I wonder how athletes train for the Olympics.

14.   Because she gave her fellow students an inspirational speech.

15.   The speech which made us all happy.

9. Fragments Test C _____

Some of the word groups below are sentences, and some are fragments. Write "correct" next to the sentences. Then revise the fragments to form complete sentences.

1. Creating a new password for my student network account was easy.

2. Taking a cruise to Alaska to see the glaciers.

3. The book that we just finished.

4. People who wanted tickets to the afternoon show.

5. Please skip to the next question.

6. Snowboarding being a dangerous sport.

7. Because my friend's notebook fell in the mud, she borrowed one of mine.

8. When the audience has gone and the theater seats are empty.

9. With a better computer, I could do my work faster.

10. Answer the questions at the end of the essay for extra practice.

11. Because I can remember most of the basic formulas.

12. Whether he drives with us or not doesn't matter.

13. Whenever I proofread my own essays.

14. Walking through the desert was a little scary.

15. If we rented a hotel room with a view of the Eiffel Tower.

10. Run-On Sentences   Test A

Some of the sentences below are correctly punctuated, and some are run-ons. Write "correct" next to the sentences with proper punctuation. Then correct each run-on sentence by making one of the independent clauses a dependent clause or by adding a comma, a *fanboys* and a comma, or a semicolon. Remember that a run-on includes two independent clauses without proper punctuation between them.

1.   I finally went to the dentist and she found a cavity in one of my teeth.

2.   We saved enough money for our trip and contacted the travel agent.

3.   Air fares go up and down, but people will always buy tickets.

4.   Someone on the bus didn't feel well so the bus driver stopped.

5.   Most people laughed when they heard the joke I didn't get it.

6.   First the phone rang then the doorbell rang.

7.   Is the critical thinking class a requirement or an elective?

8.   I finished my paper now I can focus on my chart.

9.   They met each other at a party and quickly became business partners.

10.   There are many types of computer paper; I never know what kind to buy.

11.   I practiced my speech for an hour then I went to a movie as a reward.

12.   The field trip starts at 7:00 a.m. and it lasts until 5:00 p.m.

13.   Tourists love pigeons, yet local residents often hate them.

14.   I ordered a baked potato but the server brought me fries instead.

15.   I visit the post office as often as I visit the bank.

10. Run-On Sentences Test B _____

Some of the sentences below are correctly punctuated, and some are run-ons. Write "correct" next to the sentences with proper punctuation. Then correct each run-on sentence by making one of the independent clauses a dependent clause or by adding a comma, a *fanboys* and a comma, or a semicolon. Remember that a run-on includes two independent clauses without proper punctuation between them.

1. There were cakes and pastries in the bakery window but there were no cookies.

2. Anyone can volunteer to read children stories at the new library let's do it!

3. We have changed our topic, so now we have to start over again.

4. Typically, people wear black to see a play and red to see an opera.

5. Low prices at warehouse stores tempt shoppers to spend more money.

6. The sun was shining and the birds were singing in the trees; spring had arrived.

7. Then a few clouds rolled in and we all became depressed.

8. Are you a cat person or are you a dog person?

9. The fire alarm rang so we grabbed our backpacks and walked out to the parking lot.

10. I would like to go to the party, but I have to work that weekend.

11. Scripts from famous movies are valuable collectibles yet they're hard to find.

12. Indoor plants need more care than outside plants do.

13. We stayed at the new lodge the old one has lost its charm.

14. The executives flew to the convention however, their employees drove to it.

15. I collect autographs consequently, I go to a lot of movie premieres.

10.   Run-On Sentences   Test C   _____

Some of the sentences below are correctly punctuated, and some are run-ons. Write "correct" next to the sentences with proper punctuation. Then correct each run-on sentence by making one of the independent clauses a dependent clause or by adding a comma, a *fanboys* and a comma, or a semicolon. Remember that a run-on includes two independent clauses without proper punctuation between them.

1.   You make the plane reservation and I'll buy some luggage.

2.   Fresh blueberries are delicious frozen blueberries are good, too.

3.   Fill out an application and send it in before the deadline.

4.   We locked the cabin before we went to the ski lift.

5.   Apartments and condominiums are similar in design but they are different in purpose.

6.   There are many kinds of digital cameras choosing the perfect one is difficult.

7.   Do we need a reservation or can we just walk in and pick out a rental car?

8.   Let's celebrate your promotion by going out to dinner.

9.   We saw the dinosaur bones and the Egyptian artifacts I liked the artifacts better.

10.   We read the novel then we saw the movie and wrote a comparison of the two.

11.   A bell is a friendly sound a buzzer, on the other hand, is an irritating noise.

12.   The students in my tennis class are very athletic; we all enjoy a good workout.

13.   I wear a uniform to work, so I like to dress creatively for school.

14.   A cell phone interrupted the performance and made the actors very angry.

15.   They tried to finish their essays but they were too tired.

11.   Standard English Verbs and Verb Phrases   Test A _____

<u>Double underline</u> all verbs and verb phrases in the following sentences. Remember that a verb is only one word, but a verb phrase consists of at least one helping verb (such as *have*, *has*, *will*, *is*, *were*, and *could*) and a main verb (in this test, usually a form of *send*). Also remember that the parts of a verb phrase can be interrupted by an adverb (such as *already*, *recently*, and *often*), which should not be double underlined.

1.   I usually send out several greeting cards every year.

2.   My friends and relatives sent me many cards during the holidays.

3.   I will probably send some of them my email address.

4.   For the past two years, I have sent an e-card to my boss for her birthday.

5.   I had already sent her the latest card before I noticed an error in it.

6.   I will have sent my boss twenty e-cards by the time I retire.

7.   Just as a precaution, I am currently sending out résumés.

8.   My mom was sending me a birthday gift each year until I asked her to stop.

9.   I will be sending a résumé to my favorite retail store.

10.   I have been sending encouragement cards to my sister for years.

11.   My brother has been sending me a lot of emails lately.

12.   I had been sending cards to too many relatives before I realized the expense.

13.   By the time I retire, I will have been sending my boss e-cards for twenty years.

14.   I could send her a real card once in a while for variety.

15.   Invitations to the company picnic were recently sent to all employees.

11. Standard English Verbs and Verb Phrases Test B _____

Circle the correct verb form in parentheses to match the rest of the sentence.

1. Students have (began, begun) final exams.

2. She (used, use) to ask a lot of questions during class.

3. Her teacher has (promise, promised) to write her a letter of recommendation.

4. They were (suppose, supposed) to meet in the cafeteria at noon.

5. My books were (laying, lying) on the reference desk in the library.

6. We smiled when we (saw, seen) our graduation presents.

7. You have (be, been) very busy with your club activities lately.

8. Every Monday, he would (chose, choose) one of our essays to read aloud.

9. The coach is (met, meeting) with the parents on Saturday.

10. The two of us have (plan, planned) several parties together.

11. I remember my high school reunion whenever I (hear, heard) that song.

12. The students in the quad (was, were) resting in the shade.

13. They (use, used) antique brick on the chimney because the owners wanted it.

14. I've (been hoping, was hoping) for a chance to talk to my boss about a raise.

15. Security officers turned people away because the crowd had (became, become) too big.

11. Standard English Verbs and Verb Phrases   Test C   _____

Double underline all verbs and verb phrases in the following sentences. Remember that neither the "to___" form of a verb nor the "ing" form without a helping verb can ever be a real verb in a sentence. Also, there may be more than one verb or verb phrase in each sentence. This test will be a challenge.

1. All of the players were trying to talk to the coach at the same time.
2. We had a good discussion and left the classroom with a positive attitude.
3. Board games have become popular again because families are spending more time together.
4. Have you heard the rumor that campus parking will be free next semester?
5. She has spoken to me before about the missing textbook.
6. I should have taken more science classes when I was in high school.
7. She will not be taking the test with the rest of us.
8. They both want to be millionaires before they reach thirty.
9. My speech had just started as my friends entered the auditorium.
10. Liquor companies have been beginning to advertise on television again.
11. We will have been standing in line for three hours by the time the tickets go on sale.
12. Now I understand how many problems just one mistake can cause.
13. By the time his train arrives in Denver, I will have driven all the way home.
14. People are always telling me to stand up straight.
15. One of my sisters has seen that movie sixteen times and plans to see it again.

12. Subject-Verb Agreement   Test A

_____

Circle the correct verb in parentheses to maintain subject-verb agreement.

1. Transporting ice cream cakes (is, are) difficult.

2. A history class and a math class (is, are) all I need to transfer.

3. On the floor of the classroom (was, were) her driver's license.

4. Neither of them (has, have) been to the dentist in a year.

5. Each of the students (was, were) given the same topic.

6. My neighbor and my cousin (is, are) roommates at the university.

7. A fire alarm and a car alarm (was, were) going off at the same time.

8. A vase of flowers (make, makes) any room more pleasant.

9. All of the teachers, students, and administrators (was, were) standing on the lawn.

10. The tenants and the landlord (disagree, disagrees) about the new lease contract.

11. Either the landlord or the tenants (need, needs) to compromise.

12. Either the tenants or the landlord (need, needs) to compromise.

13. Playing any musical instrument (take, takes) a lot of practice.

14. The teacher of my philosophy class never (talk, talks) about politics.

15. Therefore, the students in my philosophy class never (talk, talks) about politics.

12.   Subject-Verb Agreement   Test B   _____

Circle the correct verb in parentheses to maintain subject-verb agreement.

1.   There (was, were) a bunch of bananas on top of his car.

2.   A list of office numbers (is, are) posted on the wall in the lobby.

3.   That (is, are) only one of the reasons for my decision.

4.   The first one of my pages (was, were) stuck in the zipper of my backpack.

5.   Either your thesis or your topic sentences (need, needs) revision.

6.   The pancakes and the bacon (taste, tastes) so good at that restaurant.

7.   Your ideas (sound, sounds) very reasonable to me.

8.   One of my sisters (write, writes) for the local newspaper.

9.   Each of the tables (has, have) a centerpiece for the guests to take home.

10.   Movies with too much violence (make, makes) me depressed.

11.   Drinking too many beers definitely (has, have) its drawbacks.

12.   Most parents of a teenager (learn, learns) how to help the teen through trial and error.

13.   Poker games (has, have) been gaining popularity around the country.

14.   Cars like the ones in that movie (isn't, aren't) being built anymore.

15.   Either the hen or her chicks (was, were) making a strange noise.

12. Subject-Verb Agreement   Test C   _____

Circle the correct verb in parentheses to maintain subject-verb agreement.

1. The sign on the path (say, says), "Keep off the grass."

2. The landlord and the other tenants (seem, seems) nice.

3. One of those coins (has, have) a picture of Elvis on it.

4. Every chapter in my math book (end, ends) with a practice test.

5. Buying devices to make life easier (has, have) become an obsession for some people.

6. Sometimes, a whole box of sodas (cost, costs) as much as one six-pack.

7. One of my books (is, are) missing its cover.

8. Being on a winning team (was, were) one of her dreams.

9. Either you or I (are, am) going to Europe with the school orchestra.

10. Part-time teachers often (work, works) at more than one school.

11. (Do, Does) she have the car keys, or (do, does) you have the car keys?

12. Leaves (cover, covers) our lawn in fall; snow (cover, covers) our lawn in winter.

13. Daffodils (bloom, blooms) around the edges of our lawn in spring, and an inflatable pool (sit, sits) in the middle of our lawn in summer.

14. The bill and a signed check (was, were) in the envelope, but there (was, were) no stamp on it.

15. The lines (form, forms) the shape of a dollar sign when the dots (is, are) connected.

13. Shift in Time or Person   Test A   _____

Many of the sentences below contain shifts in time or person or use *you* inappropriately. Write "correct" next to the sentences that do not contain shifts or inappropriate *you*s. Then revise the remaining sentences to eliminate these errors.

1. People need to work hard if you want to save money for retirement.

2. Your speech covered a lot of good points, but they aren't well organized.

3. My sandwich had a piece of plastic in it, and I almost ate it.

4. Real friends tell each other the truth even when it was easier to stay quiet.

5. As soon as I walked into the house, I see a large birthday cake with my name on it.

6. All of the students who are graduating should order your caps and gowns soon.

7. He likes to sit in his hot tub, but it wasn't good for his health.

8. I rewrite my essays whenever the teacher allowed me to.

9. Someone in the back of the room said, "You asked that question already."

10. Whenever I drove home at dusk, the sun gets in my eyes, and I can't see.

11. Shopping for items online is easy once you understand the process.

12. He tried to find acting jobs, but he isn't disciplined enough.

13. When people smoke, you endanger other people's health along with your own.

14. As soon as I got out of the car, you could see the damage to the bumper.

15. While our teacher was lecturing, another teacher comes in and asks him to be quiet.

13. Shift in Time or Person   Test B

_____

Many of the sentences below contain shifts in time or person or use *you* inappropriately. Write "correct" next to the sentences that do not contain shifts or inappropriate *you*s. Then revise the remaining sentences to eliminate these errors.

1. There are fluorescent lights in the hallways and incandescent lights in the offices.

2. At that hotel, if someone sneezes, you hear it in the next room.

3. The photocopier broke down yesterday, and it is still hasn't been repaired.

4. I asked a question, and you could see that the tutor knew the answer right away.

5. The six-packs were on sale, but only if you bought a case of them.

6. To look at my mother, one wouldn't expect that she has earned a black belt in karate.

7. The guide at the museum led us into the portrait gallery and then changes his mind and moves us on to the landscape room.

8. She was born in 1960, so she is starting to feel old.

9. You wouldn't believe how expensive that couch was!

10. The students read each other's essays, and then they make suggestions.

11. A hike on that trail is easy for most people if they pack enough snacks to eat on the way.

12. The author tells the story of a whole family as they coped with their mother's illness.

13. I have learned that you can't predict success.

14. When someone wants to make a big entrance at a party, you should dress elegantly and arrive late.

15. The store closed early, so I was unable to pick up my computer.

13. Shift in Time or Person   Test C   _____

Many of the sentences below contain shifts in time or person or use *you* inappropriately. Write "correct" next to the sentences that do not contain shifts or inappropriate *you*s. Then revise the remaining sentences to eliminate these errors.

1. They requested a permit to build a new garage, but the city denied it.

2. Tomorrow you can send your broken dishes back to the factory.

3. Whenever I went to the writing center, the tutors ask to see my student identification card.

4. My drawing class met on the lawn today so that we can sketch the mountains.

5. Finding a job isn't hard; finding a job that pays well is almost impossible.

6. Once someone has a child of your own, you will understand your parents better.

7. The little girl raced down the sidewalk on a scooter and nearly knock me over.

8. When a person retires, they often go through a depression at first.

9. Many children go to summer camps and had very pleasant experiences.

10. My coffee was cold, but the microwave oven was broken, so I drink cold coffee.

11. I was called in for jury duty, but I was not chosen for a case.

12. As I stopped at the intersection, another driver pulls up behind me and honks his horn.

13. Now I know what the problem with my thesis was, so I can fix it.

14. Whenever I give a speech, you can't believe how embarrassed I feel.

15. We went to our auto club office and pick up a map for our upcoming trip to Idaho.

14. Misplaced and Dangling Modifiers Test A _____

Many of the sentences below contain misplaced or dangling modifiers. Write "correct" next to any sentences that do not contain faulty modifiers. Then revise the remaining sentences to eliminate these errors.

1. We want to sell our condo in the city and move to a house in the suburbs.

2. After seeing that movie, steak didn't sound good for dinner.

3. To design an effective logo, the message must be clear.

4. Having received the award, her speech was pulled out of her pocket.

5. Once thawed, you can add the strawberries to the whipped cream.

6. I saw an ambulance looking through the window onto the street below.

7. By numbering the items in an outline, they are easier to see.

8. Preparing for the sad film, I put a handkerchief in my pocket.

9. She sent a card to her friend over the Internet.

10. Jogging around the block, cars stopped to look at the students from the P.E. class.

11. Students in the science class were planting a garden in their street clothes.

12. I found a twenty dollar bill looking through my sister's wallet.

13. Hearing everyone start to sing, the birthday boy hid under the table.

14. The other children kept the party going by blowing out the candles on his cake.

15. She walked into the classroom with a confident smile.

14. Misplaced and Dangling Modifiers   Test B   _____

Many of the sentences below contain misplaced or dangling modifiers. Write "correct" next to any sentences that do not contain faulty modifiers. Then revise the remaining sentences to eliminate these errors.

1. I knew the man who was speaking at the podium.

2. While staying at my uncle's cabin, a snowstorm trapped us for four days.

3. At the age of nine, my parents bought me my first chemistry set.

4. There is a note for the plumber on the dishwasher.

5. At exactly two o'clock, we sat down at our desks and began to take the test.

6. I turned my essay in to the teacher that I had just finished proofreading.

7. To spell better, writers need to keep track of their own misspelled words.

8. After making the same mistake twice, a misspelled word should be memorized.

9. My presentation lasted for ten minutes, which seemed like ten hours.

10. Jammed with cans of food, I handed the heavy box to the next volunteer.

11. Talking to the actors after the performance, we learned a lot more about the play.

12. Only two weeks old, we found an abandoned puppy in the alley.

13. While zipping up my backpack, my books spilled out all over my desk.

14. At ninety-eight pounds, I need to put my dog on a diet.

15. I'll do the best that I can without a calculator on the test.

14. Misplaced and Dangling Modifiers Test C _____

Many of the sentences below contain misplaced or dangling modifiers. Write "correct" next to any sentences that do not contain faulty modifiers. Then revise the remaining sentences to eliminate these errors.

1. Ponchos look great on people with lots of fringe.

2. Twirling a baton looks easy but takes a lot of practice.

3. I watched a movie about samurai warriors relaxing in my hotel room.

4. After signing the lease, my apartment seemed much smaller than before.

5. Before burning, I raised the handle on the toaster, and my toast popped up.

6. Once you have your diploma, will you frame it?

7. Grabbing my stuff, the bus almost took off without me.

8. The children played with the marbles sitting in small groups.

9. Written in a short time, I appreciated the story's concentrated power.

10. Opening the carton, the food from the deli had an odd smell.

11. Looking ridiculous, I watched my father show off his disco moves.

12. Feeling unlucky, we canceled our plane tickets to Las Vegas.

13. All of the students got their essays back at the same time.

14. That bathing suit would look better with a tan.

15. Between our two houses is a fence about five feet high.

15. Parallel Structure   Test A   _____

The following sentences all contain parallel structures. Put { } around the parallel structures in each sentence. Remember that parallel structures are used in pairs or lists of words, phrases, or clauses. Parallel structures do not have to be exactly the same length.

1. Our hotel room in London felt small, stuffy, and damp.

2. Yesterday he needed a bike; today he needs a car.

3. The banquet room can be rented by the hour, by the day, or by the week.

4. Drivers have two options: leave early and be on time or leave on time and be late.

5. I am a better singer than she is, but she is a better composer than I am.

6. The room, the time, and the teacher were all misprinted in the catalog.

7. I had not only a broken calculator but also a number four pencil.

8. I will make either a cake or a pie for the party.

9. I will either make a cake or buy a cake for the party.

10. A headache can be an inconvenience or a symptom of a serious problem.

11. The hardest parts of the driving test involve exiting driveways, changing lanes, and making left turns.

12. On Friday, we can turn in our journals, our quiz booklets, or our homework folders.

13. My parents allowed neither pets nor plants in the house.

14. Now that she has bifocals, Traci can read recipes, newspaper articles, cereal boxes, medicine labels—anything with writing on it.

15. He knew that he needed to save for a new car and that he wanted to buy a convertible.

15. Parallel Structure   Test B

_____

Many of the sentences below contain errors in parallel structure. Write "correct" next to the sentences with matching parallel structures. Then revise the remaining sentences to eliminate errors in parallel structure.

1. I spend most of my weekends doing laundry and keep up with the yard work.

2. Hiking, camping, and fishing all require a love of the outdoors.

3. The parents were told to listen to each student's performance, to take pictures if they wanted, and applaud for everyone at the end.

4. The cafeteria sells croissants that are plain, have cream cheese, and ones with chocolate inside.

5. The review noted that the acting was dull, the script was weak, and the editing was off.

6. High schools, community colleges, and universities at the state level are all suffering from budget cuts.

7. The teacher has to decide whether to give us an extension or whether he should accept our rough drafts.

8. Ants have invaded the school kitchen inside the cupboards and the countertops.

9. She went to the airport and picked up her brother then drove him to his meeting.

10. The drywall is eight feet long, four feet in width, and it's about one inch deep.

11. Today's test was shorter, clearer, and easier than yesterday's.

12. I not only want a job, but also I need a job.

13. Bradley wants to sit in the coffee shop, look out the window, and to draw all day.

14. Rude drivers don't seem to think about others, nor do they seem to care.

15. The teacher said that our speech was well-planned, well-rehearsed, and that the presentation was strong also.

15. Parallel Structure   Test C   _____

Many of the sentences below contain errors in parallel structure. Write "correct" next to the sentences with matching parallel structures. Then revise the remaining sentences to eliminate errors in parallel structure.

1. My new year's resolutions included exercising more often and not to worry so much.

2. The dancers were tall, strong, and talented.

3. I want a career that will let me travel around the world, manage my own time, and one that will let me retire at an early age.

4. My toolbox contains the following items: a hammer, two kinds of screwdrivers, a wrench, assorted nails and screws, a pencil, and a measuring tape.

5. You can buy this fabric by the foot, by the yard, or a whole bolt of it.

6. I know someone who doesn't eat meat or dairy products and avoids wheat too.

7. By the time I get home, I have worked for four hours, studied for one hour, and attended class for three hours.

8. Applicants for the position of security officer needed prior experience and hours that needed to be flexible.

9. To need something and wanting it are two different things.

10. I would compare the blue of your eyes to the sky, but his eyes are more the color of the ocean.

11. Couldn't you tell that I was busy and that I didn't want to be disturbed?

12. She uses mugs for coffee and cups for tea.

13. We must choose either to take our two weeks of vacation now or losing it altogether.

14. On Tuesdays, I work late, but the boss lets me go home early on Thursdays.

15. Schools and factories have many things in common.

16. Pronouns   Test A

_____

Circle the correct pronoun in the parentheses.

1. It was (he, him) who left early.

2. (He, Him) and his son are both coming with us.

3. The instructor gave extra help to both (she and I, her and me).

4. Neither the tutor nor the students will be taking (her, their) ten-minute break today.

5. Neither the students nor the tutor will be taking (her, their) ten-minute break today.

6. Tina is younger than (I, me).

7. (We, Us) students are concerned about recent events.

8. The financial aid office awarded grants to Cheryl and (I, me).

9. All of the jurors had (his, their) own reasons for the verdict.

10. (They and we, Them and us) have different ideas about teamwork.

11. The cashier handed Sandy and (I, me) our tickets to the concert.

12. The manager should give a raise to (she and I, her and me).

13. The librarian demonstrated the new research method for the teacher and (we, us).

14. Each of the twins does (his, their) own homework.

15. Carla asked if my mother and (I, me) could drive her to the bank.

16. Pronouns   Test B

_____

Circle the correct pronoun in the parentheses.

1. (You and I, You and me) should study together more often.

2. Did you know that the tutor is older than (I, me)?

3. Just between (you and I, you and me), I think we go to a good school.

4. My dentist and (I, me) have the same last name.

5. A travel warning was given to (we, us) tourists at the airport.

6. You received higher grades than (I, me) last semester.

7. The book that (you and she, you and her) are sharing needs to be returned to the library.

8. A person in a ghost costume handed my kids and (I, me) a bag of candy.

9. Everyone knows that the one who has sacrificed the most is (she, her).

10. Either the dancers or the choreographer will take (his, their) bow first.

11. Either the choreographer or the dancers will take (his, their) bow first.

12. The coach gave a look of encouragement to (she and I, her and me) that I'll never forget.

13. It was (he, him) who named the horse Lucky.

14. The ones who should be sorry are (they, them).

15. No other team has members that are more motivated than (we, us).

16. Pronouns Test C _____

Circle the correct pronoun in the parentheses.

1. The party at fault in the accident was (I, me).

2. That secret should be kept between (you and I, you and me).

3. Each of the contestants in the reality series had (his or her, their) own fan club.

4. (We, Us) students feel strongly about the open-door policy.

5. The boss gave raises to three employees—Jay, Wendy, and (I, me).

6. Three employees—Jay, Wendy, and (I, me)—received raises from the boss.

7. Last week, (he and she, her and him) drove to yoga class with us.

8. Last week, we drove to yoga class with (he and she, him and her).

9. A credit card company sent offers to my brother and (I, me).

10. The children in the class baked a cake for (you and I, you and me).

11. No one has seen that movie as many times as (I, me).

12. (He and she, Him and her) are going with us to Las Vegas.

13. Are those your books? Yes, those are (they, them).

14. It was (she, her) who wrote the essay that the teacher read in class.

15. May I speak with Anthony? Yes, this is (he, him).

17. Commas Test A   _____

Add commas to the following sentences according to the first set of comma rules, those that show how commas are used to separate elements. Remember to add commas here for three reasons: 1) to separate two independent clauses joined by a *fanboys*; 2) to separate items in a series or items in dates and addresses; and 3) to separate introductory (or tag) words, phrases, and clauses from the rest of the sentence.

1. Whenever I hear that song I think of my graduation from high school.

2. The picture frame on his desk isn't sterling silver is it?

3. Business envelopes come in different sizes colors and finishes.

4. In May 2004 they became partners in an online business.

5. My thesis is strong but I need more support from the book.

6. I wanted to speak to the manager not her assistant.

7. After the meeting with our insurance agent we added more coverage to our policy.

8. Someone asked the speaker a question but he didn't have time to answer it.

9. Our debate team traveled to the tournament and we finished in second place.

10. Until you asked me that question I had never considered a new major.

11. Taking a terrible risk I swerved into the carpool lane to avoid hitting a piece of metal.

12. The list of ingredients for the chili includes beans tomatoes green onions white onions garlic and bell peppers.

13. The loaf of bread was brand new yet it looked moldy to me.

14. My imaginary address in high school was 101 Fake St. Nowhere Ohio and I wish I still lived there.

15. We must start a savings account for we have such exciting travel plans.

17. Commas Test B

Add commas to the following sentences according to the second set of comma rules, those that show how commas are used to enclose "scoopable" elements within a sentence. Remember that scoopable elements include names of people being spoken to, interrupting expressions, and unnecessary additional information. Scoopable elements require commas before and after them to show that the enclosed information can be left out. Some sentences are correct.

1. My computer an old laptop is still useful for typing papers at school.

2. I have it seems forgotten to set the machine to record.

3. The musical <u>The Phantom of the Opera</u> was a huge success on stage.

4. The movie however did not make much money.

5. Jess the assistant manager wants the manager's job.

6. The scholarship that I applied for was awarded to someone else.

7. Mr. Yates the new principal urged the parents to join the PTA.

8. Our campus believe it or not is going to be in a commercial for candy bars.

9. The science textbook that we use has too many pictures of snakes in it.

10. The anaconda one of the biggest snakes has a whole chapter devoted to it.

11. We know Joan that you did not mean to hurt anyone's feelings.

12. The straps of her backpack the one she bought in Paris finally disintegrated.

13. Pepperoni and mushrooms my favorite pizza toppings are the most popular toppings of all.

14. I know a pizza restaurant that uses barbecue sauce instead of pizza sauce.

15. We would like to point out Mr. Hopkins that you have neglected to pay your bill.

17. Commas   Test C   _____

Add all of the necessary commas to the following sentences. Be sure to have a reason for every comma you add. Some sentences are correct.

1. Talking in a lower voice than usual he appeared tired.

2. Under the new sod was a layer of fertilizer.

3. Wednesday March 22 2003 was the day we met.

4. The sand blew across the tennis court and got in our eyes.

5. Ms. Scantron one of the substitutes took the class to the library.

6. The mayor's car believe it or not is a tiny two-seater.

7. When will you graduate Inez?

8. My mother sister-in-law and niece attended the awards banquet.

9. Well it did sound like a good idea didn't it?

10. Even though it rained last week the drought continues in parts of the state.

11. That I believe was a trick question.

12. The teacher arranged our desks in a circle sat in the middle and led the discussion.

13. As their show dogs pranced into the arena the breeders beamed with pride.

14. The breeders beamed with pride as their show dogs pranced into the arena.

15. Running for office takes planning patience funding and luck.

18. Semicolons, Colons, and Dashes   Test A   _____

Add missing semicolons, colons, and dashes to the following sentences. Be sure to have a reason for every mark you add. Any commas already within the sentences are necessary and should not be changed. Some sentences are correct.

1. I haven't finished my research paper therefore, I need to go to the library.

2. He was sixty-five years old yesterday at least I think that's how old he was.

3. The roses are blooming the days are getting hotter summer is here.

4. That couch comes in five colors beige, brown, blue, green, and heather gray.

5. If you come on the hike with us, you should bring a hat, sunblock, water, and a snack.

6. The puppy was afraid of our cat at first now they are best friends.

7. Most plants will thrive if they have the following necessities air, water, and sunlight.

8. I had my carpets cleaned on the day of the party what a mistake!

9. You have studied algebra therefore, you should know about variables.

10. We have decided on a name for our new canary Hello Yellow.

11. That was a great movie it should have won the Best Picture award.

12. I am believe it or not planning to swim with sharks on my vacation.

13. I had never seen alligators up close before they were really interesting.

14. The clouds disappeared as the sun came up it was a perfect day.

15. This medication should not be taken by anyone with the following symptoms hives, shortness of breath, or itchy scalp.

18. Semicolons, Colons, and Dashes   Test B   _____

Add missing semicolons, colons, and dashes to the following sentences. Be sure to have a reason for every mark you add. Any commas already within the sentences are necessary and should not be changed. Some sentences are correct.

1. My brother hates to sing, but he actually has a really good voice.

2. The salmon company has decided on a new image for its labels a silvery sunset reflecting on the ocean.

3. He was old enough to buy beer however, he had left his driver's license at home.

4. Here are the ingredients for the lemon bars flour, butter, sugar, eggs, and lemon juice.

5. A broken pipe flooded our basement we had to use fans day and night to dry all the woodwork.

6. The proctor will provide scratch paper you should bring your own pencil and eraser, however.

7. Besides an applicant's work experience, hiring committees focus on two things the interview and the letters of recommendation.

8. Someone called the police therefore, we had to turn down our party music.

9. Volunteers handed bags of groceries to the next person in line at the relief center.

10. Juan Carlos is an excellent violinist, and think of it he taught himself.

11. The paint is peeling on that old car he wants to buy the windshield is cracking, too.

12. The valedictorian started her speech by quoting from Emerson's "Self-Reliance."

13. Our teacher walks in every day and says the following words "Hi, everyone. How's it goin'?"

14. It was a mistake a big mistake to ask my dad if he was in a bad mood.

15. Midterm exams begin next Monday I've already started studying for them.

18.   Semicolons, Colons, and Dashes   Test C   _____

Add missing semicolons, colons, and dashes to the following sentences. Be sure to have a reason for every mark you add. Any commas already within the sentences are necessary and should not be changed. Some sentences are correct.

1.   I blurted out my password in the middle of class what an idiot!

2.   Leave a one-inch margin around your essay to leave room for the teacher's markings.

3.   Here's a suggestion for anyone going to their concert bring earplugs if you ever want to hear again.

4.   We watched taffy being pulled and caramel apples being dipped it was fun!

5.   We have taken many classes together our favorite, however, was a first-aid class.

6.   The car would not start its battery was dead.

7.   The ring master always opened the circus with these words "Ladies and gentlemen, boys and girls. . . ."

8.   The recipients of the awards were two students from our class Austin and Jay.

9.   My little brother has inherited two thousand dollars from our aunt however, my parents are not going to tell him until he is eighteen.

10.   We can identify essay types in addition, we know how to write them ourselves.

11.   The gardener's tools all of them were stolen from the back of his truck.

12.   I made a poster, a model, and a handout to help with my DNA presentation.

13.   I finally got the news I had been waiting for my sister had a baby, and she named it after me.

14.   That truck comes with the following standard equipment power steering, air-conditioning, and power windows.

15.   What kind of sandwich do you like roast beef, ham, turkey, or the vegetarian special?

19. Periods, Question Marks, Exclamation Points, _____ Quotation Marks, Underlining (*Italics*), and Capital Letters   Test A

Add end punctuation—periods, questions marks, and exclamation points—to the following sentences. Look within the sentences for abbreviations or quotations that may also need these marks. Any punctuation already used within the sentences is correct and should not be changed. Pay close attention to the use of quotation marks, underlining, and capitals so that you can add them to the next test.

1. Mr Wright teaches four math classes in fall and three English classes in spring

2. We asked the caterer how many people the cake served

3. We celebrated St Patrick's Day in New York City last year

4. "How old are you" the doorman at the nightclub asked

5. The children watching the puppet show shouted "Boo" at the mean wizard

6. One of the most powerful movies I've ever seen is <u>In the Heat of the Night</u>

7. I liked the title of my essay about dolphins; I called it "Beauty Isn't Only Fin Deep"

8. My sister never read the book <u>Orlando</u>, but she saw the movie and liked it

9. In my parents' day, a famous burger campaign asked, "Where's the beef"

10. Our subscription to <u>TV Guide</u> runs out next month, doesn't it

11. "The Happiest Place on Earth" is Disneyland's slogan

12. Novelist William S. Burroughs said, "You can't fake quality any more than you can fake a good meal"

13. When my dad told my mom about the car's bumper, she laughed

14. When Dad told Mom about the car's bumper, did she laugh

15. I wonder if back-to-school week is a depressing time for parents, too

19. Periods, Question Marks, Exclamation Points, _____

Quotation Marks, Underlining (*Italics*), and Capital Letters   Test B

Where necessary, add quotation marks, underlining (*italics*), and capital letters to the following sentences. Remember to put quotation marks around someone's exact words. Also, put quotation marks around titles of shorter works, and underline (or *italicize*) titles of longer works. Any punctuation already in the sentences is correct. Pay close attention to the use of periods, question marks, and exclamation points used with quotation marks and underlining so that you can add them all to the next test.

1.   composer gustav mahler said, if you think you're boring your audience, go slower not faster.

2.   alice walker was the first black woman to win the pulitzer prize for fiction.

3.   tom cruise yells show me the money! in the movie jerry maguire.

4.   cheer up, philander chase johnson once wrote, the worst is yet to come.

5.   stevie smith begins one of her poems, why is the word pretty so underrated?

6.   mary wollstonecraft said, independence [is] the basis of every virtue.

7.   in the animated shrek movies, eddie murphy plays the role of donkey.

8.   i want you home by midnight, my dad warned.

9.   jerome k. jerome wrote that love is like the measles; we all have to go through it.

10.   in the movie version of grease, john travolta sings the song greased lightnin'.

11.   gertrude stein described her approach to writing this way: i write for myself and strangers.

12.   the book who moved my cheese? became well-known because of its title.

13.   the line success is counted sweetest begins one of emily dickinson's most famous poems.

14.   oscar wilde said this about truth: the truth is rarely pure, and never simple.

15.   shakespeare's play twelfth night begins with a shipwreck.

19. Periods, Question Marks, Exclamation Points, _____

Quotation Marks, Underlining (*Italics*), and Capital Letters   Test C

Where necessary, add periods, question marks, exclamation points, quotation marks, underlining (*italics*), and capital letters to the following sentences. Any punctuation already in the sentences is correct.

1.   may i see your car registration the officer asked

2.   karen bought the soundtrack to the movie the royal tenenbaums

3.   the people at the front of the line shouted, stop pushing

4.   we saw the matrix and the matrix reloaded, but we skipped the matrix revolutions

5.   my sister has been reading the series of books called redwall by brian jacques

6.   in class today, we read the declaration of independence aloud

7.   in the old movie if i had a million, wc fields buys cars and crashes them for fun

8.   crimes of the heart is a great play by beth henley; it was a good movie, too

9.   i read the ancient greek play oedipus rex in high school

10.   athens, greece, hosted the 2004 summer olympics

11.   i forget that labor day is in september; i always think, for some reason, that it is in may

12.   johnny depp stars in the film versions of the disney attraction pirates of the caribbean

13.   did he say, i need my book every day or i read my book every day

14.   her favorite season is spring because of the flowers

15.   i took a class called basic grammar, and i learned a lot

20. Posttest Part A

_____

Circle the correct word in each set of parentheses.

1. Attendance in the lab will (affect, effect) the overall grade.

2. The new statue in the park already has a chip in (it's, its) base.

3. It's hotter inside (than, then) outside today.

4. On my short drive to work, I go (passed, past) four fast-food restaurants.

5. The twins have the same goal; (their, there, they're) both planning to be doctors.

6. I feel (bad, badly) about skipping my parents' anniversary party.

7. Sometimes it's fun to listen to other (people's, peoples') cell phone conversations.

8. We should (have, of) called the airport before we left home.

9. When I got back from my trip, all of my mail was (lying, laying) on the welcome mat.

10. You were (suppose, supposed) to take the other freeway to avoid traffic.

11. That company sells online as well as (threw, through) its mail-order catalog.

12. She has (saw, seen) that movie several times.

13. The dentists in that building (has, have) reserved all the best parking spaces.

14. Invitations to our graduation (was, were) mailed out on Friday.

15. A key ring and a cell phone (was, were) turned in to campus police.

16. I know that Carl has studied more than (I, me).

17. For (we, us) tenants on the third floor, the stairs are a nuisance.

18. Only two students—Sandra and (I, me)—got an A on the test.

19. My friend and (I, me) will meet you at the fountain in front of the theater.

20. Can we keep that information just between you and (I, me)?

20.   Posttest   Part B

_____

Each of the following sentences demonstrates an error listed below. Identify the error by placing the appropriate letter in the blank. Then revise the sentence to correct the error.

    a. misused adjective or adverb
    b. fragment
    c. run-on sentence
    d. subject-verb agreement error
    e. shift in time or person
    f. misplaced or dangling modifier
    g. faulty parallel structure

21. ___ Running to catch the plane, a security guard stopped me to check my passport.

22. ___ We all did good on the quiz last week.

23. ___ When the fire alarm rings and everyone walks out into the hallways.

24. ___ My plans for spring break include tennis, golf, and playing poker.

25. ___ Driving real slow can be as dangerous as driving real fast.

26. ___ I have taken the two required music classes but I want to take more.

27. ___ Writing is hard for some people; you definitely need confidence to do it well.

28. ___ The fall semester will be short this year there will be more holidays than usual.

29. ___ The birds in the tree behind my house makes a lot of noise in the morning.

30. ___ While we were watching the movie, my friend's phone rings and ruins the scene.

20. Posttest Part C   _____

Rewrite the following sentences to include the necessary punctuation
(, ; : . ! ? ' " " ___) and capital letters.

31. i wanted to get a job on campus but all of the good ones have been taken

32. as we were walking down the sidewalk someone behind us shouted look out

33. i took ms smiths drawing class because a friend of mine said it was great

34. most high school students have read the short story the lottery by shirley
    jackson

35. we saw the los angeles womens shakespeare company perform hamlet in 1995

36. have there been any changes in your taxes this year my accountant asked

37. mom dad and i stood together at the bottom of the statue of liberty and looked up

38. the television series desperate housewives became an instant success

39. the judge made the following statement the ticket you received was a mistake

40. the hendersons garden looks beautiful dont you think

Answers

1. Pretest   Part A

1. then
2. They're
3. than
4. its
5. lying
6. good
7. brothers'
8. couldn't
9. help
10. used
11. gone
12. are
13. offer
14. have
15. are
16. me
17. he
18. she
19. us
20. I

1. Pretest   Part B

Possible revisions are *italicized*.

21. e. (shift in time) As I was driving home from work, my sister *called* me on my cell phone.
22. b. (fragment) Students who participate in class and do their homework on time *should succeed*.
23. c. (run-on sentence) The deadline was approaching, but we shortened our outlines and finished on time.
24. a. (misused adjective form) Our room at the ski lodge was the *largest* of the three.
25. d. (subject-verb agreement error) My counselor *understands* some of the problems I have.
26. e. (shift in person) I don't understand some of my friends; *I* never know what they're thinking.
27. g. (faulty parallel structure) This room needs better windows, more desks, and *a thorough cleaning*.
28. b. (fragment) *I will take* as much time as necessary on each of the test questions.
29. a. (misused adverb) They felt *bad* about forgetting my birthday.
30. f. (dangling modifier) Without a jacket, *I was freezing due to the wind*.

1. Pretest   Part C

31. I don't know whether I should apply for a loan or not.
32. Mr. Branford always writes positive comments on my homework.
33. She has read the book <u>The House on Mango Street</u> four times.
34. A person who was born before 1990 can still qualify for that license.
35. Janet, who was born on February 10, 1989, can still qualify for that license.
36. Will you figure out the taxes this year, or do you want me to do it?
37. Katharine Lee Bates wrote the words to "America the Beautiful."
38. Whenever my mom gets home from work, she smiles in a special way.
39. A basic first-aid kit has the following items: bandages, medicines, and instructions.
40. The children's center is next to the women's gym.

2. Words Often Confused   Test A

1. an, a
2. advice, accept
3. affect, effects
4. all ready, our
5. break, brakes
6. chose, clothes
7. course, coarse
8. choose, complement
9. a, compliment
10. conscience, its
11. desert, dessert
12. feel, due
13. have, forth
14. it's, here
15. new, know

2. Words Often Confused   Test B

1. lead, loose
2. led, past
3. personnel, personal
4. peace, there
5. principal, quite
6. write, right
7. Their, than
8. there, then
9. threw, through
10. too, two, to
11. whether, where

12. Whose, wear
13. woman, who's
14. passed, your
15. You're

2. Words Often Confused   Test C

1. Due, weather
2. are, effects
3. They're, fourth
4. desert, its
5. chose, their
6. woman, lose
7. have, your
8. advise, to
9. It's, quiet
10. except, whose
11. an, it's
12. brakes, were
13. two, then
14. complimented, write
15. passed, past

3. Parts of Speech   Test A

   pro   v   adj n prep   n
1. I researched my topic on the Internet.

      pro prep   n   v   adj n
2. Everyone on the team has the same goal.

      adj n v adv adj prep   n
3. The post office is very busy during the holidays.

   pro v   pro   prep adj   n
4. I met someone from my hometown.

     n conj n   v   adv   adj
5. Coffee and tea taste completely different.

    pro adv v adj   adj   n
6. You always tell such interesting stories.

    pro v   conj pro v   adj n
7. I laugh whenever I remember that scene.

        n   prep   n prep   n   v   adj   n

8.   The people at the back of the line shared a pepperoni pizza.

            adj   n   v   adj   n

9.   The library steps need a better railing.

    pro v conj   n   v   adv

10.   I hope that the weather improves soon.

         n   prep n v adj   n

11.   Walking to school is good exercise.

         n   v   adv   prep   n conj pro   v prep n

12.   Frank sleeps better during the day, so   he works at night.

    interj adj n   v   adv v   adj   n

13.   No, my car does not need new tires.

         n   adv   v   adv

14.   Happiness usually arrives unexpectedly.

    pro   v   adj adj   n   prep adj   n

15.   We found two baby squirrels in a hollow log.

3. Parts of Speech   Test B

        n   v   adj   adj   n

1.   Tennis is a popular outdoor sport.

    adj   adj   n   v   adj   n

2.   His English teacher assigned a research paper.

      n   conj   n   v adv adj n prep   n

3.   Movies and television are only two forms of entertainment.

    adj   n   v prep adj   adj   n prep pro

4.   One pickle tastes like every other pickle to   him.

      adv   adj   n   v prep   n

5.   The highly polished silverware sparkled on the table.

    conj   n   v   n   v prep   n

6.   While the children played, the adults talked about politics.

    pro v   v   n prep   n   conj   adj   n

7.   They will accept a letter of recommendation or a personal essay.

<pre>
       adj   n   v   v prep   adj   n
8.   Five people were sitting in the waiting room.
</pre>

<pre>
          n   v   v   adj   n   prep   n
9.   Scientists have discovered new information about dinosaurs.
</pre>

<pre>
      v pro v pro adj   n conj   n
10. Did you send him a real letter or an email?
</pre>

<pre>
      adj   n   v   v   adv   adj   adv
11. Paper money has become more colorful recently.
</pre>

<pre>
     interj adj   n   v pro adj   n
12. Ouch! That application gave me a paper cut.
</pre>

<pre>
      n conj   n   v conj pro v prep   n
13. Hal and Trudy sang as they drove up the coast.
</pre>

<pre>
      pro   v   v prep n   adv   adv
14. We should go on picnics more often.
</pre>

<pre>
      adj   adj   n v adv adv adj prep adj   n
15. That restaurant's food is much too spicy for most people.
</pre>

3. Parts of Speech   Test C

<pre>
       adj   n   v   n   prep   n   conj prep   n
1.   Heavy rains caused flooding in the valleys and in the mountains.
</pre>

<pre>
      adj   n   v   adv adj n conj adj   adj   n
2.   Our uniforms included light gray pants and simple white shirts.
</pre>

<pre>
       pro   v   conj n conj n   v   n
3.   Everyone knows that blue and yellow make green.
</pre>

<pre>
      n   v   v   adj   adj   n
4.   Lisa has become a well-known pastry chef.
</pre>

<pre>
      n v   adv   adj   adj   n
5.   A smile is a very revealing facial expression.
</pre>

<pre>
       n   v   n   pro v adv v conj v adj   adj   n
6.   Vegans are vegetarians who do not eat or use any animal products.
</pre>

<pre>
        n   prep   adj   n   v   adj n
7.   The students in the singing class sang a new song.
</pre>

```
          adv  pro  v  pro  adv
8.   Then they sang it again.

          pro  prep adj  n    v    n prep    n
9.   Everyone on  our block has a party in the summer.

        pro  v   v  prep pro conj pro  v  adj    n
10.  You can travel with  us  if   you get your passport.

        adj      n    v   v  adv  adj
11.  European vacations can be very expensive.

         n      adv    v      adj    n
12.  Jonathan quietly answered the doctor's questions.

         n     v     n  prep adj   n   prep adj n
13.  Candice received a basket of gourmet foods for  her birthday.

         adj    n    v  prep    n  conj   n    v
14.  The football players ran onto the field as the music played.

       adj  n   v    v   prep n prep   adj     n
15.  Ten people were standing in line at the Indian restaurant.
```

4. Adjectives and Adverbs   Test A

1. adjective
2. adverb
3. adjective
4. adverb
5. adjective
6. adverb
7. adjective
8. adjective
9. adjective
10. adverb
11. adverb (*Early* modifies the adjective *warning*, not the noun *system*.)
12. adjective
13. adjective
14. adverb
15. adverb

4. Adjectives and Adverbs   Test B

1. adjective
2. adverb
3. adjective

4. adverb
5. adjective
6. adjective
7. adverb
8. adjective
9. adjective
10. adjective
11. adverb
12. adjective
13. adjective
14. adverb
15. adverb

4. Adjectives and Adverbs   Test C

     adj   adv adj
1.   My counselor is a very nice person.

     adj   adv   adj
2.   Our teacher usually begins the class with a short lecture.

     adj   adj   adj
3.   Fancy mice can be good pets for some people.

      adj   adv adj
4.   The next train leaves in exactly ten minutes.

      adj   adv adj
5.   The peach pie was too sweet for me.

     adj   adj   adj   adj
6.   One ticket to that amusement park costs fifty dollars.

          adv   adj   adj
7.   I became extremely sleepy during the piano recital.

       adv   adj adj   adj   adv
8.   He does not have any clear transfer plans yet.

     adj   adj   adj   adj
9.   The room's furniture included one couch, two chairs, and a coffee table.

     adv adj   adj
10. The lime green curtains gave the room an eerie glow.

     adv   adj   adv adv
11. I always reply to your emails very quickly.

      adj adj adj

12. Do you want our old air conditioner?

      adj   adv adj

13. The morning air felt so crisp in the mountains.

   adj adj   adj   adj adj

14. My cell phone is smaller than your cell phone.

       adj adj

15. Jake has the tiniest cell phone of all.

5. Contractions and Possessives Test A

1. Who's
2. its
3. they're
4. it's
5. puppy's
6. You're
7. it's
8. their
9. people's
10. Children's
11. girls'
12. mail carrier's
13. your
14. aren't
15. men's

5. Contractions and Possessives Test B

1. book's, its
2. They're, their
3. house's, its
4. cousin's (or cousins' if more than one owns the car), it's
5. Who's, company's
6. friend's, didn't
7. It's, countries'
8. boys', girls'
9. Men's, women's
10. teacher's, its
11. students', their
12. semester's, isn't
13. You're, who's
14. don't, whose
15. week's, teacher's

5. Contractions and Possessives   Test C

1.   its, *it's*
2.   *They're*, their
3.   dad's, *it's*
4.   Cats', *aren't*
5.   judge's (or judges' if more than one made the decision), *wasn't*
6.   *I'm*, its
7.   *They've*, students'
8.   *couldn't*, brother's
9.   *There's*, Smiths'
10. *wasn't*, teacher's
11. athlete's, *should've*
12. *You're*, whose
13. *What's*, Tomlins'
14. *could've*, school's
15. city's, *isn't*

6. Subjects and Verbs   Test A

1.   <u>I</u> <u>wrote</u> several new entries in my journal.
2.   <u>She</u> <u>takes</u> two classes and <u>works</u> part-time.
3.   A <u>box</u> of paper <u>sat</u> in the hallway for three days.
4.   At the beginning of the semester, <u>students</u> <u>wait</u> in long lines at the bookstore.
5.   Our remote <u>control</u> <u>fell</u> under the couch and <u>disappeared</u>.
6.   <u>Bowling</u> <u>is</u> very good exercise.
7.   The <u>library</u> <u>contains</u> books, magazines, newspapers, and other formats of information.
8.   Canned <u>pineapple</u>, <u>pears</u>, and <u>peaches</u> <u>taste</u> delicious at any time of year.
9.   <u>Many</u> of my friends <u>call</u> me on the weekends.
10. Without instructions, <u>they</u> <u>assembled</u> the cabinet and <u>placed</u> their television on top of it.
11. <u>We</u> <u>studied</u> together and <u>talked</u> about life.
12. <u>All</u> of the tables <u>have</u> six chairs.
13. The school's new <u>schedule</u> <u>is</u> an improvement.
14. <u>We</u> <u>listened</u> to the speaker and <u>took</u> notes in the dark.
15. The <u>desks</u> and the <u>chalkboard</u> <u>are</u> clean but <u>need</u> repair.

6. Subjects and Verbs   Test B

1.   Under the porch <u>sat</u> a little lost <u>dog</u>.
2.   There <u>are</u> two <u>methods</u> for payment.
3.   <u>Cheese</u> <u>is</u> a popular snack at parties.
4.   [<u>You</u>] <u>Mail</u> me one copy of the receipt.
5.   Here <u>are</u> several <u>photos</u> from the reunion.
6.   There <u>is</u> a good <u>reason</u> for his behavior.
7.   Inside the shop <u>was</u> a beautiful <u>assortment</u> of pastries.

8. [You] Gather your notes for our meeting.
9. There were two boats on the lake today.
10. Towels in hotels are always too small.
11. [You] Be careful with your passwords.
12. That is a classic yoga exercise.
13. Near the window stood two artificial potted plants.
14. [You] Knead the bread dough for eight minutes.
15. [You] Sort all of the files alphabetically.

6. Subjects and Verbs   Test C

1. His high school math teacher lives next door to him.
2. There are several buildings with balconies on our block.
3. People abandoned their cars in the traffic jam.
4. [You] Look under the welcome mat for the key to my house.
5. Adults and children require different doses of medicine.
6. [You] Take the freeway to its end and turn left.
7. Someone's alarm rang all night and bothered everyone in the neighborhood.
8. Inside the plastic bags were several kinds of snacks.
9. There is a full moon in the sky tonight.
10. Sugar, butter, and flour are the only ingredients in the dough.
11. [You] Send me an email tomorrow.
12. A lizard jumped off a rock and scared the hikers.
13. Six of the twelve eggs broke in the pan.
14. Drawing and singing are two very admirable talents.
15. [You] Toast the marshmallows slowly for the fullest flavor.

7. Phrases   Test A

1. Examples and charts (in textbooks) can be very helpful.
2. We met (at a conference) (about safety).
3. The last part (of his address) causes confusion (for everyone).
4. (For dinner) (on Sunday), they ate hamburgers (with fries).
5. Yesterday, she and I took the placement test together. *no prepositional phrases*
6. Thanksgiving is the last Thursday (in November).
7. He spoke (to me) quietly (during the film).
8. (After the fire drill), everyone met (in the cafeteria) (for coffee).
9. I feel too vulnerable (without a service contract) (for my computer).
10. I acted (as the judge) (in a mock trial) (at my school).
11. Customers sit (on benches) (at that restaurant).
12. A blimp hovered (in the sky) (above the football stadium).
13. I found the expiration date (on the bottom) (of the can).
14. Words (in one language) often sound (like words) (in other languages).
15. The front (of that phone) opens (with a little click).

7. Phrases   Test B

1. He <u>enjoys</u> [playing the guitar].
2. They <u>need</u> [to complete their applications].
3. [Taken by a professional photographer], the graduation pictures <u>pleased</u> everyone.
4. I <u>saw</u> my friend [waiting in line at the gas station].
5. Most people <u>like</u> [to receive compliments].
6. However, [receiving gifts] <u>makes</u> some people uncomfortable.
7. She really <u>wants</u> [to support the team].
8. [Choosing the right major] <u>takes</u> time.
9. They <u>tried</u> [to improve their credit score].
10. I sometimes <u>visualize</u> us [traveling across Europe].
11. The students [chosen for that project] <u>were</u> the best.
12. [Built in 1951], our house <u>is</u> in vogue right now.
13. I <u>want</u> [to walk a lot before my trip].
14. We <u>ate</u> our individual pizzas slowly, [enjoying every bite].
15. Olympic athletes <u>love</u> [to get gold medals].

7. Phrases   Test C

1. I <u>like</u> [to have a break (between classes)].
2. [Helped (by the teacher's assistant)], the students <u>did</u> well (on that essay).
3. We <u>went</u> home (without [taking any pictures (of the volcano)]).
4. My family <u>needs</u> [to watch less television (during the week)].
5. [Eaten (in large quantities)], black licorice <u>can be</u> dangerous.
6. [Seen (from a distance)], the clouds <u>seemed</u> small and harmless.
7. (In the first paragraph), <u>try</u> [to state your main idea].
8. I <u>like</u> [going (to the movies) (with my friends)].
9. You <u>deserve</u> an award (for [following the directions so closely]).
10. The object (of the game) <u>is</u> [to score the highest number (of points)].
11. He <u>enjoys</u> [making his own bread] and [sharing it (with others)].
12. The pictures [taken (by that photographer)] <u>were</u> the best (in the gallery).
13. [Written (in pencil)], the letter <u>was</u> difficult [to read (without a strong light)].
14. [Loaded (with vitamin C)], tomatoes <u>are</u> good (for most people).
15. [Given a real bath (by the kennel staff)], my dog <u>looked</u> clean and <u>smelled</u> fresh.

8. Clauses   Test A

1. <u>Whenever Ms. Stark asks a question</u>, she looks at the ceiling.
2. He dropped his biology class <u>because it conflicted with his work schedule</u>.
3. I know <u>what you mean</u>.
4. We liked the movie <u>until we read the review</u>.
5. <u>When she eats shrimp</u>, she sometimes has an allergic reaction.
6. The athlete <u>who wins the most medals</u> gets the most television coverage.
7. <u>As the actor turned toward the audience</u>, he sneezed.

8. Someone <u>who knows your password</u> accessed your email yesterday.
9. Professor Talbot, <u>whom we all know</u>, received an award.
10. <u>Before the curtain opens</u>, someone checks all of the scenery.
11. She noticed <u>that the corner of the couch had a rip at the bottom</u>.
12. The party was a success <u>because the guests knew each other well</u>.
13. <u>After the rainy season ends</u>, the weather here is perfect.
14. I know many people <u>who exercise regularly</u>.
15. Do you know <u>where their house is</u>?

8. Clauses   Test B

1. <u>As I ate my lunch at the park</u>, a bird <u>that lived in a tree</u> flew down onto my bench.
2. Do you know anyone <u>who builds kitchen cabinets</u>?
3. <u>Because he needed the key to the classroom</u>, the substitute called the security office.
4. <u>Wherever we went in Paris</u>, we saw dogs <u>who reminded us of our puppy back at home</u>.
5. Nobody knows <u>who took the basket</u>.
6. Many people wish <u>that they lived at a different time in history</u>.
7. I saw that movie <u>when I was in elementary school</u>.
8. The homework <u>that we had last week</u> was actually fun.
9. <u>Unless it rains on Sunday</u>, the field trip will proceed <u>as we planned</u>.
10. One helicopter landed on top of the mountain just <u>as another one took off</u>.
11. The bells ring only <u>while classes are in session</u>.
12. <u>After I took a nap</u>, I felt so much better <u>that I finished all of my homework</u>.
13. You are taller <u>than I am</u>, and she is taller <u>than you are</u>.
14. <u>Although I know that I can't afford it</u>, I want to take a trip around the world.
15. Professional actors and musicians never give up <u>once they have begun a performance</u>.

8. Clauses   Test C

1. In high school, I wrote an essay <u>that won an award</u>.
2. <u>Once he received his tickets</u>, he exchanged them for seats <u>that were closer to the stage</u>.
3. During the debate, I supported <u>whatever my team proposed</u>.
4. The novel <u>that we read</u> includes several characters <u>who change for the better</u>.
5. People <u>who read newspapers</u> know more about the candidates <u>who are on the ballot</u>.
6. No one shares his time more freely <u>than he does</u>.
7. Everyone noticed <u>that the scenery was stuck</u> and <u>that the actors were nervous</u>.
8. <u>Until the rain arrives</u>, we should use sprinklers <u>that are controlled by a timer</u>.
9. <u>Whenever I need extra money</u>, I work more hours.
10. The tuxedos <u>that we rented</u> required a large deposit <u>because they were fancy</u>.

11. Ice dancing is a sport that demands both physical ability and courage.
12. Since you missed class last week, you are a little behind on the project that we started.
13. We will be satisfied with whatever happens because we know that we studied.
14. Many believe that horses know when a person is afraid.
15. Since I love to drive, I am glad that long road trips are popular again.

9. Fragments   Test A

Possible revisions are *italicized*.

1. *I ate* too many sweets during the holidays.
2. correct
3. *We read a book by* that famous writer with the unusual name.
4. Because of the cold weather and the harsh winds, *my skin is dry.*
5. correct
6. *These are* the most comfortable chairs in their whole house.
7. The newest pens with erasable ink *work much better than the old ones.*
8. correct (The sentence is a command; the subject *You* is understood.)
9. *The parking situation caused* a lot of problems for people at the concert.
10. correct
11. Creating stencil designs on my computer *is fun.*
12. The stairs in the library and the ramps in the parking structure *are too steep.*
13. correct
14. correct
15. Peaches and pears *are* summer fruits.

9. Fragments   Test B

Student revisions may differ.

1. Organic eggs are now available in most stores.
2. correct
3. The substitute teacher gave the test.
4. In the morning when the sun shines, I listen to my favorite radio shows.
5. correct
6. When I was a volunteer, I helped with the relief efforts.
7. When you write an essay based on sources from the library or the Internet, always keep hard copies of everything.
8. correct
9. We had a parakeet when I was growing up.
10. I can't wait until the semester is over and I get my final grades.
11. correct (The sentence is a command; the subject *You* is understood.)
12. No one knows why mosquitoes are attracted to some people more than others.
13. correct
14. She gave her fellow students an inspirational speech.
15. The result made us all happy.

9. Fragments   Test C

Possible revisions are *italicized*.

1. correct
2. *We took* a cruise to Alaska to see the glaciers.
3. The book that we just finished *was interesting*.
4. People who wanted tickets to the afternoon show *couldn't get them*.
5. correct (The sentence is a command; the subject *You* is understood.)
6. Snowboarding *is* a dangerous sport.
7. correct
8. When the audience has gone and the theater seats are empty, *I sit on the stage and dream*.
9. correct
10. correct (The sentence is a command; the subject *You* is understood.)
11. Because I can remember most of the basic formulas, *I do well on math tests*.
12. correct
13. Whenever I proofread my own essays, *I can't find the mistakes*.
14. correct
15. If we rented a hotel room with a view of the Eiffel Tower, *it would cost too much*.

10. Run-On Sentences   Test A

Student revisions may differ.

1. I finally went to the dentist, and she found a cavity in one of my teeth.
2. correct
3. correct
4. Someone on the bus didn't feel well, so the bus driver stopped.
5. Most people laughed when they heard the joke, *but* I didn't get it.
6. First the phone rang; then the doorbell rang.
7. correct
8. I finished my paper; now I can focus on my chart.
9. correct
10. correct
11. I practiced my speech for an hour; then I went to a movie as a reward.
12. The field trip starts at 7:00 a.m., and it lasts until 5:00 p.m.
13. correct
14. I ordered a baked potato, but the server brought me fries instead.
15. correct

10. Run-On Sentences   Test B

Student revisions may differ.

1. There were cakes and pastries in the bakery window, but there were no cookies.
2. Anyone can volunteer to read children stories at the new library; let's do it!
3. correct
4. correct

5. correct
6. The sun was shining, and the birds were singing in the trees; spring had arrived.
7. Then a few clouds rolled in, and we all became depressed.
8. Are you a cat person, or are you a dog person?
9. The fire alarm rang, so we grabbed our backpacks and walked out to the parking lot.
10. correct
11. Scripts from famous movies are valuable collectibles, yet they're hard to find.
12. correct
13. We stayed at the new lodge; the old one has lost its charm.
14. The executives flew to the convention; however, their employees drove to it.
15. I collect autographs; consequently, I go to a lot of movie premieres.

10. Run-On Sentences   Test C

Student revisions may differ.

1. You make the plane reservation, and I'll buy some luggage.
2. Fresh blueberries are delicious; frozen blueberries are good, too.
3. [*You*] Fill out an application, and [*you*] send it in before the deadline. *or* correct
4. correct
5. Apartments and condominiums are similar in design, but they are different in purpose.
6. There are many kinds of digital cameras; choosing the perfect one is difficult.
7. Do we need a reservation, or can we just walk in and pick out a rental car?
8. correct
9. We saw the dinosaur bones and the Egyptian artifacts; I liked the artifacts better.
10. We read the novel; then we saw the movie and wrote a comparison of the two.
11. A bell is a friendly sound; a buzzer, on the other hand, is an irritating noise.
12. correct
13. correct
14. correct
15. They tried to finish their essays, but they were too tired.

11. Standard English Verbs and Verb Phrases   Test A

1. I usually <u>send</u> out several greeting cards every year.
2. My friends and relatives <u>sent</u> me many cards during the holidays.
3. I <u>will</u> probably <u>send</u> some of them my email address.
4. For the past two years, I <u>have sent</u> an e-card to my boss for her birthday.
5. I <u>had</u> already <u>sent</u> her the latest card before I <u>noticed</u> an error in it.
6. I <u>will have sent</u> my boss twenty e-cards by the time I <u>retire</u>.
7. Just as a precaution, I <u>am</u> currently <u>sending</u> out résumés.
8. My mom <u>was sending</u> me a birthday gift each year until I <u>asked</u> her to stop.
9. I <u>will be sending</u> a résumé to my favorite retail store.
10. I <u>have been sending</u> encouragement cards to my sister for years.
11. My brother <u>has been sending</u> me a lot of emails lately.

12. I <u>had been sending</u> cards to too many relatives before I <u>realized</u> the expense.
13. By the time I <u>retire</u>, I <u>will have been sending</u> my boss e-cards for twenty years.
14. I <u>could send</u> her a real card once in a while for variety.
15. Invitations to the company picnic <u>were</u> recently <u>sent</u> to all employees.

11. Standard English Verbs and Verb Phrases   Test B

1. begun
2. used
3. promised
4. supposed
5. lying
6. saw
7. been
8. choose
9. meeting
10. planned
11. hear
12. were
13. used
14. been hoping
15. become

11. Standard English Verbs and Verb Phrases   Test C

1. All of the players <u>were trying</u> to talk to the coach at the same time.
2. We <u>had</u> a good discussion and <u>left</u> the classroom with a positive attitude.
3. Board games <u>have become</u> popular again because families <u>are spending</u> more time together.
4. <u>Have</u> you <u>heard</u> the rumor that campus parking <u>will be</u> free next semester?
5. She <u>has spoken</u> to me before about the missing textbook.
6. I <u>should have taken</u> more science classes when I <u>was</u> in high school.
7. She <u>will</u> not <u>be taking</u> the test with the rest of us.
8. They both <u>want</u> to be millionaires before they <u>reach</u> thirty.
9. My speech <u>had</u> just <u>started</u> as my friends <u>entered</u> the auditorium.
10. Liquor companies <u>have been beginning</u> to advertise on television again.
11. We <u>will have been standing</u> in line for three hours by the time the tickets <u>go</u> on sale.
12. Now I <u>understand</u> how many problems just one mistake <u>can cause</u>.
13. By the time his train <u>arrives</u> in Denver, I <u>will have driven</u> all the way home.
14. People <u>are</u> always <u>telling</u> me to stand up straight.
15. One of my sisters <u>has seen</u> that movie sixteen times and <u>plans</u> to see it again.

12. Subject-Verb Agreement   Test A

1. is
2. are
3. was

4. has
5. was
6. are
7. were
8. makes
9. were
10. disagree
11. need
12. needs
13. takes
14. talks
15. talk

12. Subject-Verb Agreement   Test B

1. was
2. is
3. is
4. was
5. need
6. taste
7. sound
8. writes
9. has
10. make
11. has
12. learn
13. have
14. aren't
15. were

12. Subject-Verb Agreement   Test C

1. says
2. seem
3. has
4. ends
5. has
6. costs
7. is
8. was
9. am
10. work
11. Does, do
12. cover, covers
13. bloom, sits
14. were, was
15. form, are

13. Shift in Time or Person   Test A

Possible revisions are *italicized.*

1. People need to work hard if *they* want to save money for retirement.
2. Your speech covered a lot of good points, but they *weren't* well organized.
3. correct
4. Real friends tell each other the truth even when it *is* easier to stay quiet.
5. As soon as I walked into the house, I *saw* a large birthday cake with my name on it.
6. All of the students who are graduating should order *their* caps and gowns soon.
7. He likes to sit in his hot tub, but it *isn't* good for his health.
8. I rewrite my essays whenever the teacher *allows* me to.
9. correct
10. Whenever I *drive* home at dusk, the sun gets in my eyes, and I can't see.
11. correct
12. He *tries* to find acting jobs, but he isn't disciplined enough.
13. When people smoke, *they* endanger other people's health along with *their* own.
14. As soon as I got out of the car, *I* could see the damage to the bumper.
15. While our teacher was lecturing, another teacher *came* in and *asked* him to be quiet.

13. Shift in Time or Person   Test B

Possible revisions are *italicized.*

1. correct
2. At that hotel, if someone sneezes, *people* hear it in the next room.
3. correct
4. I asked a question, and *I* could see that the tutor knew the answer right away.
5. correct
6. correct
7. The guide at the museum led us into the portrait gallery and then *changed* his mind and *moved* us on to the landscape room.
8. correct
9. *That couch was very expensive*!
10. correct
11. correct
12. The author tells the story of a whole family as they *cope* with their mother's illness.
13. I have learned that *I* can't predict success.
14. *Someone who wants to make* a big entrance at a party should dress elegantly and arrive late.
15. correct

13. Shift in Time or Person   Test C

Possible revisions are *italicized*.

1. correct
2. correct
3. Whenever I *go* to the writing center, the tutors ask to see my student identification card.
4. My drawing class met on the lawn today so that we *could* sketch the mountains.
5. correct
6. Once *you have* a child of your own, you will understand your parents better.
7. The little girl raced down the sidewalk on a scooter and nearly *knocked* me over.
8. When *people retire*, they often go through a depression at first.
9. Many children go to summer camps and *have* very pleasant experiences.
10. My coffee was cold, but the microwave oven was broken, so I *drank* cold coffee.
11. correct
12. As I stopped at the intersection, another driver *pulled* up behind me and *honked* his horn.
13. Now I know what the problem with my thesis *is*, so I can fix it.
14. When I give a speech, *I feel really embarrassed*.
15. We went to our auto club office and *picked* up a map for our upcoming trip to Idaho.

14. Misplaced and Dangling Modifiers   Test A

Possible revisions are *italicized*.

1. correct
2. *After I saw that movie*, I didn't want steak for dinner.
3. *An effective logo must have a clear message.*
4. Having received the award, *she pulled her speech out of her pocket*.
5. Once thawed, *the strawberries can be added* to the whipped cream.
6. *As I looked through the window onto the street below*, I saw an ambulance.
7. *Numbered items in an outline* are easier to see.
8. correct
9. She sent *her friend a card over the Internet*.
10. *Drivers stopped their cars to look at the P.E. students jogging around the block.*
11. *Wearing their street clothes*, students in the science class were planting a garden.
12. *Looking through my sister's wallet*, I found a twenty dollar bill.
13. correct
14. correct
15. correct

14. Misplaced and Dangling Modifiers   Test B

Possible revisions are *italicized*.

1. correct
2. While *we were* staying at my uncle's cabin, a snowstorm trapped us for four days.
3. *When I was* nine, my parents bought me my first chemistry set.
4. correct (or) *On the dishwasher,* there is a note for the plumber.
5. correct
6. *Right after I had finished proofreading my essay, I turned it in* to the teacher.
7. correct
8. After making the same mistake twice, *a writer should memorize a misspelled word.*
9. correct
10. I handed the heavy box, *jammed with cans of food,* to the next volunteer.
11. correct
12. We found an abandoned *two-week-old* puppy in the alley.
13. While *I was* zipping up my backpack, my books spilled out all over my desk.
14. At ninety-eight pounds, *my dog needs to be put on a diet.*
15. *Without a calculator,* I'll do the best that I can on the test.

14. Misplaced and Dangling Modifiers   Test C

Possible revisions are *italicized*.

1. Ponchos *with lots of fringe* look great on people.
2. correct
3. *Relaxing in my hotel room,* I watched a movie about samurai warriors.
4. After *I signed* the lease, my apartment seemed much smaller than before.
5. Before *my toast burned,* I raised the handle on the toaster, and my toast popped up.
6. correct
7. *As I grabbed my stuff,* the bus almost took off without me.
8. *Sitting in small groups,* the children played with the marbles.
9. Written in a short time, *the story had a concentrated power that I appreciated.*
10. Opening the carton, *I noticed that* the food from the deli had an odd smell.
11. Looking ridiculous, *my father showed off* his disco moves.
12. correct
13. correct
14. That bathing suit would look better *on someone* with a tan.
15. correct

15. Parallel Structure   Test A

1. Our hotel room in London felt {small}, {stuffy}, and {damp}.
2. {Yesterday he needed a bike}; {today he needs a car}.
3. The banquet room can be rented {by the hour}, {by the day}, or {by the week}.
4. Drivers have two options: {leave early and be on time} or {leave on time and be late}.

5. {I am a better singer than she is}, but {she is a better composer than I am}.
6. {The room}, {the time}, and {the teacher} were all misprinted in the catalog.
7. I had not only {a broken calculator} but also {a number four pencil}.
8. I will make either {a cake} or {a pie} for the party.
9. I will either {make a cake} or {buy a cake} for the party.
10. A headache can be {an inconvenience} or {a symptom of a serious problem}.
11. The hardest parts of the driving test involve {exiting driveways}, {changing lanes}, and {making left turns}.
12. On Friday, we can turn in {our journals}, {our quiz booklets}, or {our homework folders}.
13. My parents allowed neither {pets} nor {plants} in the house.
14. Now that she has bifocals, Traci can read {recipes}, {newspaper articles}, {cereal boxes}, {medicine labels}—anything with writing on it.
15. He knew {that he needed to save for a new car} and {that he wanted to buy a convertible}.

15. Parallel Structure   Test B

Possible revisions are *italicized*.

1. I spend most of my weekends doing laundry and *keeping* up with the yard work.
2. correct
3. The parents were told to listen to each student's performance, to take pictures if they wanted, and *to applaud* for everyone at the end.
4. The cafeteria sells *plain croissants, cream cheese croissants, and chocolate croissants*.
5. correct
6. High schools, community colleges, and *state universities* are all suffering from budget cuts.
7. The teacher has to decide whether to give us an extension or *to accept* our rough drafts.
8. Ants have invaded the school kitchen inside the cupboards and *on the countertops*.
9. She went to the airport, *picked up her brother, and drove him to his meeting*.
10. The drywall is eight feet long, four feet *wide*, and *one inch deep*.
11. correct
12. I not only want a job; *I also* need a job.
13. Bradley wants to sit in the coffee shop, look out the window, and *draw* all day.
14. correct
15. The teacher said that our speech was well-planned, well-rehearsed, and *well-presented*.

15. Parallel Structure   Test C

Possible revisions are *italicized*.

1. My new year's resolutions included exercising more often and not *worrying* so much.
2. correct
3. I want a career that will let me travel around the world, manage my own time, and *retire early*.

4. correct
5. You can buy this fabric by the foot, by the yard, or *by the bolt.*
6. I know someone who doesn't eat *meat, dairy products, or wheat.*
7. correct
8. Applicants for the position of security officer needed prior experience and *flexible hours.*
9. To need something and *to want it* are two different things.
10. I would compare the blue of your eyes to the sky *and the blue of his eyes to the ocean.*
11. correct
12. correct
13. We must choose either to take our two weeks of vacation now or *to lose it altogether.*
14. On Tuesdays, I work late; *but on Thursdays, I go home early.*
15. correct

16. Pronouns   Test A

1. he
2. He
3. her and me
4. their
5. her
6. I
7. We
8. me
9. their
10. They and we
11. me
12. her and me
13. us
14. his
15. I

16. Pronouns   Test B

1. You and I
2. I
3. you and me
4. I
5. us
6. I
7. you and she
8. me
9. she
10. his
11. their
12. her and me
13. he
14. they
15. we

16. Pronouns   Test C

1. I
2. you and me
3. his or her
4. We
5. me
6. I
7. he and she
8. him and her
9. me
10. you and me
11. I
12. He and she
13. they
14. she
15. he

17. Commas   Test A

1. Whenever I hear that song, I think of my graduation from high school.
2. The picture frame on his desk isn't sterling silver, is it?
3. Business envelopes come in different sizes, colors, and finishes.
4. In May 2004, they became partners in an online business.
5. My thesis is strong, but I need more support from the book.
6. I wanted to speak to the manager, not her assistant.
7. After the meeting with our insurance agent, we added more coverage to our policy.
8. Someone asked the speaker a question, but he didn't have time to answer it.
9. Our debate team traveled to the tournament, and we finished in second place.
10. Until you asked me that question, I had never considered a new major.
11. Taking a terrible risk, I swerved into the carpool lane to avoid hitting a piece of metal.
12. The list of ingredients for the chili includes beans, tomatoes, green onions, white onions, garlic, and bell peppers.
13. The loaf of bread was brand new, yet it looked moldy to me.
14. My imaginary address in high school was 101 Fake St., Nowhere, Ohio, and I wish I still lived there.
15. We must start a savings account, for we have such exciting travel plans.

17. Commas   Test B

1. My computer, an old laptop, is still useful for typing papers at school.
2. I have, it seems, forgotten to set the machine to record.
3. correct
4. The movie, however, did not make much money.
5. Jess, the assistant manager, wants the manager's job.
6. correct

7. Mr. Yates, the new principal, urged the parents to join the PTA.
8. Our campus, believe it or not, is going to be in a commercial for candy bars.
9. correct
10. The anaconda, one of the biggest snakes, has a whole chapter devoted to it.
11. We know, Joan, that you did not mean to hurt anyone's feelings.
12. The straps of her backpack, the one she bought in Paris, finally disintegrated.
13. Pepperoni and mushrooms, my favorite pizza toppings, are the most popular toppings of all.
14. correct
15. We would like to point out, Mr. Hopkins, that you have neglected to pay your bill.

17. Commas Test C

1. Talking in a lower voice than usual, he appeared tired.
2. correct
3. Wednesday, March 22, 2003, was the day we met.
4. correct
5. Ms. Scantron, one of the substitutes, took the class to the library.
6. The mayor's car, believe it or not, is a tiny two-seater.
7. When will you graduate, Inez?
8. My mother, sister-in-law, and niece attended the awards banquet.
9. Well, it did sound like a good idea, didn't it?
10. Even though it rained last week, the drought continues in parts of the state.
11. That, I believe, was a trick question.
12. The teacher arranged our desks in a circle, sat in the middle, and led the discussion.
13. As their show dogs pranced into the arena, the breeders beamed with pride.
14. correct
15. Running for office takes planning, patience, funding, and luck.

18. Semicolons, Colons, and Dashes Test A

Since dashes may replace other punctuation for emphasis, student choices may vary slightly.

1. I haven't finished my research paper; therefore, I need to go to the library.
2. He was sixty-five years old yesterday—at least I think that's how old he was.
3. The roses are blooming; the days are getting hotter: (or ;) summer is here.
4. That couch comes in five colors: beige, brown, blue, green, and heather gray.
5. correct
6. The puppy was afraid of our cat at first; now they are best friends.
7. Most plants will thrive if they have the following necessities: air, water, and sunlight.
8. I had my carpets cleaned on the day of the party—what a mistake!
9. You have studied algebra; therefore, you should know about variables.
10. We have decided on a name for our new canary: Hello Yellow.
11. That was a great movie; it should have won the Best Picture award.
12. I am—believe it or not—planning to swim with sharks on my vacation.

13. I had never seen alligators up close before; they were really interesting.
14. The clouds disappeared as the sun came up; it was a perfect day.
15. This medication should not be taken by anyone with the following symptoms: hives, shortness of breath, or itchy scalp.

18. Semicolons, Colons, and Dashes   Test B

Since dashes may replace other punctuation for emphasis, student choices may vary slightly.

1. correct
2. The salmon company has decided on a new image for its labels: a silvery sunset reflecting on the ocean.
3. He was old enough to buy beer; however, he had left his driver's license at home.
4. Here are the ingredients for the lemon bars: flour, butter, sugar, eggs, and lemon juice.
5. A broken pipe flooded our basement; we had to use fans day and night to dry all the woodwork.
6. The proctor will provide scratch paper; you should bring your own pencil and eraser, however.
7. Beside an applicant's work experience, hiring committees focus on two things: the interview and the letters of recommendation.
8. Someone called the police; therefore, we had to turn down our party music.
9. correct
10. Juan Carlos is an excellent violinist, and—think of it—he taught himself.
11. The paint is peeling on that old car he wants to buy; the windshield is cracking, too.
12. correct
13. Our teacher walks in every day and says the following words: "Hi, everyone. How's it goin'?"
14. It was a mistake—a big mistake—to ask my dad if he was in a bad mood.
15. Midterm exams begin next Monday; I've already started studying for them.

18. Semicolons, Colons, and Dashes   Test C

Since dashes may replace other punctuation for emphasis, student choices may vary slightly.

1. I blurted out my password in the middle of class—what an idiot!
2. correct
3. Here's a suggestion for anyone going to their concert: bring earplugs if you ever want to hear again.
4. We watched taffy being pulled and caramel apples being dipped—it was fun!
5. We have taken many classes together; our favorite, however, was a first-aid class.
6. The car would not start; its battery was dead.
7. The ring master always opened the circus with these words: "Ladies and gentlemen, boys and girls. . . ."
8. The recipients of the awards were two students from our class: Austin and Robert.

9. My little brother has inherited two thousand dollars from our aunt; however, my parents are not going to tell him until he is eighteen.
10. We can identify essay types; in addition, we know how to write them ourselves.
11. The gardener's tools—all of them—were stolen from the back of his truck.
12. correct
13. I finally got the news I had been waiting for: (or ;) my sister had a baby, and she named it after me.
14. That truck comes with the following standard equipment: power steering, air-conditioning, and power windows.
15. What kind of sandwich do you like—roast beef, ham, turkey, or the vegetarian special?

19. Periods, Question Marks, Exclamation Points, Quotation Marks, Underlining (*Italics*), and Capital Letters   Test A

1. Mr. Wright teaches four math classes in fall and three English classes in spring.
2. We asked the caterer how many people the cake served.
3. We celebrated St. Patrick's Day in New York City last year.
4. "How old are you?" the doorman at the nightclub asked.
5. The children watching the puppet show shouted "Boo!" at the mean wizard.
6. One of the most powerful movies I've ever seen is <u>In the Heat of the Night</u>.
7. I liked the title of my essay about dolphins; I called it "Beauty Isn't Only Fin Deep."
8. My sister never read the book <u>Orlando</u>, but she saw the movie and liked it.
9. In my parents' day, a famous burger campaign asked, "Where's the beef?"
10. Our subscription to <u>TV Guide</u> runs out next month, doesn't it?
11. "The Happiest Place on Earth" is Disneyland's slogan.
12. Novelist William S. Burroughs said, "You can't fake quality any more than you can fake a good meal."
13. When my dad told my mom about the car's bumper, she laughed.
14. When Dad told Mom about the car's bumper, did she laugh?
15. I wonder if back-to-school week is a depressing time for parents, too.

19. Periods, Question Marks, Exclamation Points, Quotation Marks, Underlining (*Italics*), and Capital Letters   Test B

1. Composer Gustav Mahler said, "If you think you're boring your audience, go slower not faster."
2. Alice Walker was the first black woman to win the Pulitzer Prize for fiction.
3. Tom Cruise yells "Show me the money!" in the movie <u>Jerry McGuire</u>.
4. "Cheer up," Philander Chase Johnson once wrote, "the worst is yet to come."

5. Stevie Smith begins one of her poems, "Why is the word <u>pretty</u> so underrated?"
6. Mary Wollstonecraft said, "Independence [is] the basis of every virtue."
7. In the animated <u>Shrek</u> movies, Eddie Murphy plays the role of Donkey.
8. "I want you home by midnight," my dad warned.
9. Jerome K. Jerome wrote that "Love is like the measles; we all have to go through it."
10. In the movie version of <u>Grease,</u> John Travolta sings the song "Greased Lightnin'."
11. Gertrude Stein described her approach to writing this way: "I write for myself and strangers."
12. The book <u>Who Moved My Cheese?</u> became well-known because of its title.
13. The line "Success is counted sweetest" begins one of Emily Dickinson's most famous poems.
14. Oscar Wilde said this about truth: "The truth is rarely pure, and never simple."
15. Shakespeare's play <u>Twelfth Night</u> begins with a shipwreck.

19. Periods, Question Marks, Exclamation Points, Quotation Marks, Underlining (*Italics*), and Capital Letters   Test C

1. "May I see your car registration?" the officer asked.
2. Karen bought the soundtrack to the movie <u>The Royal Tenenbaums</u>.
3. The people at the front of the line shouted, "Stop pushing!"
4. We saw <u>The Matrix</u> and <u>The Matrix Reloaded</u>, but we skipped <u>The Matrix Revolutions</u>.
5. My sister has been reading the series of books called <u>Redwall</u> by Brian Jacques.
6. In class today, we read "The Declaration of Independence" (or <u>The Declaration of Independence</u>) aloud.
7. In the old movie <u>If I Had a Million,</u> W.C. Fields buys cars and crashes them for fun.
8. <u>Crimes of the Heart</u> is a great play by Beth Henley; it was a good movie, too.
9. I read the ancient Greek play <u>Oedipus Rex</u> in high school.
10. Athens, Greece, hosted the 2004 summer Olympics.
11. I forget that Labor Day is in September; I always think, for some reason, that it is in May.
12. Johnny Depp stars in the film versions of the Disney attraction <u>Pirates of the Caribbean</u>.
13. Did he say, "I <u>need</u> my book every day?" or "I <u>read</u> my book every day?"
14. Her favorite season is spring because of the flowers.
15. I took a class called Basic Grammar, and I learned a lot.

20. Posttest Part A

1. affect
2. its
3. than
4. past
5. they're
6. bad

7. people's
8. have
9. lying
10. supposed
11. through
12. seen
13. have
14. were
15. were
16. I
17. us
18. I
19. I
20. me

20. Posttest   Part B

Possible revisions are *italicized*.

21. f. (misplaced modifier) *As I ran to catch the plane*, a security guard stopped me to check my passport.
22. a. (misused adjective) We did *well* on the quiz last week.
23. b. (fragment) When the fire alarm *rings, everyone* walks out into the hallways.
24. g. (faulty parallel structure) My plans for spring break include tennis, golf, and *poker*.
25. a. (misused adverbs) Driving *really slowly* can be as dangerous as driving *really* fast.
26. c. (run-on sentence) I have taken the two required music *classes, but* I want to take more.
27. e. (shift in person) Writing is hard for some people; *a person* definitely *needs* confidence to do it well. (or) *A good writer definitely needs confidence.*
28. c. (run-on sentence) The fall semester will be short this *year; there* will be more holidays than usual.
29. d. (subject-verb agreement error) The birds in the tree behind my house *make* a lot of noise in the morning.
30. e. (shift in time) While we were watching the movie, my friend's phone *rang* and *ruined* the scene.

20. Posttest   Part C

31. I wanted to get a job on campus, but all of the good ones have been taken.
32. As we were walking down the sidewalk, someone behind us shouted, "Look out!"
33. I took Ms. Smith's drawing class because a friend of mine said it was great.
34. Most high school students have read the short story "The Lottery" by Shirley Jackson.

35. We saw the Los Angeles Women's Shakespeare Company-perform <u>Hamlet</u> in 1995.
36. "Have there been any changes in your taxes this year? " my accountant asked.
37. Mom, Dad, and I stood together at the bottom of the Statue of Liberty and looked up.
38. The television series <u>Desperate Housewives</u> became an instant success.
39. The judge made the following statement: "The ticket you received was a mistake."
40. The Hendersons' garden looks beautiful, don't you think?